DATE DUE			
DE 8'67			
NO 10 68			
DE 26 '70			
MR 27 '70			
MAR 14 1979			
MAY 15 1986			
JUN 03 1987			
JUN 08 1987			
NOV. 22 1993			
NOV 2 2 REC'D			
MAY 1 2 2010			
FEB 01 2012			
JAN 1 2 2012			
GAYLORD			PRINTED IN U.S.A.

REGENTS RENAISSANCE DRAMA SERIES

General Editor: Cyrus Hoy
Advisory Editor: G. E. Bentley

THE FIRST PART OF HIERONIMO
and
THE SPANISH TRAGEDY

THOMAS KYD

[The Spanish Comedy, *or*]
The First Part of Hieronimo
and
The Spanish Tragedy
[*or* Hieronimo is Mad Again]

Edited by
ANDREW S. CAIRNCROSS

UNIVERSITY OF NEBRASKA PRESS · LINCOLN

Copyright © 1967 by the University of Nebraska Press
All Rights Reserved
Library of Congress Catalog Card Number: 66–20826

MANUFACTURED IN THE UNITED STATES OF AMERICA

Regents Renaissance Drama Series

The purpose of the Regents Renaissance Drama Series is to provide soundly edited texts, in modern spelling, of the more significant plays of the Elizabethan, Jacobean, and Caroline theater. Each text in the series is based on a fresh collation of all sixteenth- and seventeenth-century editions. The textual notes, which appear above the line at the bottom of each page, record all substantive departures from the edition used as the copy-text. Variant substantive readings among sixteenth- and seventeenth-century editions are listed there as well. In cases where two or more of the old editions present widely divergent readings, a list of substantive variants in editions through the seventeenth century is given in an appendix. Editions after 1700 are referred to in the textual notes only when an emendation originating in some one of them is received into the text. Variants of accidentals (spelling, punctuation, capitalization) are not recorded in the notes. Contracted forms of characters' names are silently expanded in speech prefixes and stage directions, and, in the case of speech prefixes, are regularized. Additions to the stage directions of the copy-text are enclosed in brackets. Stage directions such as "within" or "aside" are enclosed in parentheses when they occur in the copy-text.

Spelling has been modernized along consciously conservative lines. "Murther" has become "murder," and "burthen," "burden," but within the limits of a modernized text, and with the following exceptions, the linguistic quality of the original has been carefully preserved. The variety of contracted forms ('*em, 'am, 'm, 'um, 'hem*) used in the drama of the period for the pronoun *them* are here regularly given as '*em*, and the alternation between *a'th'* and *o'th'* (for *on* or *of the*) is regularly reproduced as *o'th'*. The copy-text distinction between preterite endings in -*d* and -*ed* is preserved except where the elision of *e* occurs in the penultimate syllable; in such cases, the final syllable is contracted. Thus, where the old editions read "threat'ned," those of the present series read "threaten'd." Where, in the old editions, a contracted preterite in -*y'd* would yield -*i'd* in modern spelling (as in "try'd," "cry'd," "deny'd"), the word is here given in its full form (e.g., "tried," "cried," "denied").

Punctuation has been brought into accord with modern practices. The effort here has been to achieve a balance between the generally light pointing of the old editions, and a system of punctuation which, without overloading the text with exclamation marks, semicolons, and dashes, will make the often loosely flowing verse (and prose) of the original syntactically intelligible to the modern reader. Dashes are regularly used only to indicate interrupted speeches, or shifts of address within a single speech.

Explanatory notes, chiefly concerned with glossing obsolete words and phrases, are printed below the textual notes at the bottom of each page. References to stage directions in the notes follow the admirable system of the Revels editions, whereby stage directions are keyed, decimally, to the line of the text before or after which they occur. Thus, a note on 0.2 has reference to the second line of the stage direction at the beginning of the scene in question. A note on 115.1 has reference to the first line of the stage direction following line 115 of the text of the relevant scene.

CYRUS HOY

University of Rochester

Contents

Regents Renaissance Drama Series	v
List of Abbreviations	ix
Introduction	xi
THE FIRST PART OF HIERONIMO	1
THE SPANISH TRAGEDY	55
Appendix: Chronology	177

List of Abbreviations

TEXTS

The First Part of Hieronimo

Q	Quarto, 1605

The Spanish Tragedy

Q1	Undated quarto (British Museum C.34.d.7)
MSR	Malone Society Reprint of Q1, edited by W. W. Greg and David Nichol Smith. 1948.
Q2	Quarto, 1594
Q3	Quarto, 1599
Q4	Quarto, 1602 (with "Additions")
MSR4	Malone Society Reprint of Q4, edited by W. W. Greg in consultation with F. S. Boas. 1925.
Q5	Quarto, 1603 (with colophon of that year)
Q6	Quarto, 1610 (colophon, 1611)
Q7	Quarto, 1615
Q8	Quarto, 1618
Q9	Quarto, 1623
Q10	Quarto, 1633
Qq	All the above editions

EDITIONS

D	Robert Dodsley. *A Select Collection of Old Plays*. London, 1744. Vol. II.
Hw	Thomas Hawkins. *Origin of the English Drama*. London, 1773, Vol. II.
R	Isaac Reed. *Dodsley's Old Plays*. London, 1780. Vol. III.
C	J. P. Collier. *Dodsley's Old Plays*. London, 1825. Vol. III.

LIST OF ABBREVIATIONS

Hz	W. C. Hazlitt. *Dodsley's Old Plays.* London, 1874. Vol. IV (*1 Hieronimo*) and Vol. V (*The Spanish Tragedy*)
M	J. M. Manly. *Specimens of the Pre-Shakespearean Drama.* Boston, 1897. Vol. II.
S	J. Schick, ed. *The Spanish Tragedy.* The Temple Dramatists. London, 1898.
B	F. S. Boas, ed. *The Works of Thomas Kyd.* Oxford, 1901.
E	Philip Edwards, ed. *The Spanish Tragedy.* The Revels Plays. London, 1959.
O-S	Robert Ornstein and Hazelton Spencer, eds. *Elizabethan and Jacobean Tragedy.* Boston, 1964.

GENERAL

Brereton	J. Le Gay Brereton. "Notes on the Text of Kyd," *Englische Studien,* XXXVII (1907), 87–99.
Chambers	E. K. Chambers. *The Elizabethan Stage.* Oxford, 1923.
conj.	conjecture
edd.	editors
Lamb	Charles Lamb. *Specimens of English Dramatic Poets.* London, 1854.
OED	*Oxford English Dictionary*
S.D.	stage direction
S.P.	speech prefix
Tilley	M. P. Tilley. *A Dictionary of the Proverbs of England in the Sixteenth and Seventeenth Centuries.* Ann Arbor, 1950.

Introduction

LIFE

Thomas Kyd, son of Francis Kyd, scrivener, and his wife Agnes or Anna, was baptized on November 6, 1558, in the Church of St. Mary Woolnoth, Lombard Street, London. On October 26, 1565, he was entered at the recently founded Merchant Taylors' School, under its famous headmaster, Richard Mulcaster. He was thus the schoolfellow of Edmund Spenser, and may also have been contemporary with Thomas Lodge. Although scraps of Cambridge slang occur in *The First Part of Hieronimo* (*1 Hieronimo*) there is no other evidence that he attended either university; and Nashe's attack (below, p. xxxi) suggests that, like Shakespeare, he did not. Such classical learning as he shows, he could easily have acquired at school; it is often inaccurate, like his knowledge of history, geography, French, and Italian. His use of legal terms suggests that he may have followed for a time his father's occupation. In the fifteen-eighties, he rose rapidly to fame as a dramatist, with *1 Hieronimo*, *The Spanish Tragedy*, and *Soliman and Perseda*. Though these were all published anonymously, *The Spanish Tragedy* can be ascribed from a reference in Heywood's *Apology for Actors* (1612), and the others from various links with that play.

In his Letter to Sir John Puckering, Lord Keeper of the Great Seal (that is, administrative head of the legal profession),[1] written after the death of Marlowe on June 1, 1593, Kyd speaks of having been in the service of a certain lord "almost theis vj yeres." For this lord's players Marlowe also wrote "two years synce," i.e., in 1591, at which time he and Kyd were "wrytinge in one chamber." The lord was probably Pembroke,[2] for whose company Marlowe,

---

[1] See F. S. Boas, *The Works of Thomas Kyd* (Oxford, 1901), Frontispiece, for a facsimile of Kyd's letter.

[2] See Peter Alexander, *Shakespeare's "Henry VI" and "Richard III"* (Cambridge, 1929), p. 203; and cf. C. F. Tucker Brooke, *Life of Marlowe* (London, 1930), p. 47, and F. S. Boas, *Christopher Marlowe* (Oxford, 1940) p. 242.

INTRODUCTION

exceptionally, wrote *Edward II*. It seems likely that Pembroke employed Kyd otherwise than as a dramatist—an assumption that agrees with "theis vj yeres," Kyd's turning to Italian "translations"[3] such as Tasso's *The Housholders Philosophie* (1588), and the first recorded appearance of Pembroke's Men as late as 1592. It has also been suggested, however, that Lord Strange[4] or Lord Sussex[5] may be the lord Kyd speaks of in the letter.

Kyd's career was interrupted on May 12, 1593, by his arrest on a "libell that concernd the State"[6]—possibly in connection with bills set up on the walls of the Dutch churchyard in Austin Friars, and elsewhere. His rooms were searched and among his papers was found part of a theological "disputation" which had been "shufled with some of myne (vnknowne to me)," and for which he was accused of atheism—actually a form of Unitarianism was involved. Marlowe was himself arrested a week later. Kyd was tortured, but maintained his innocence on both counts. As a result, however, he lost his position, and Puckering appears to have remained deaf to an appeal for his influence with the "Lord." In his search for patronage, Kyd dedicated his translation of Garnier's *Cornélie* to the Countess of Sussex early in 1594. The Dedication promised a future translation of Garnier's *Portia*. It was never fulfilled, for he died towards the end of the year.[7]

THE SPANISH PLAYS

Kyd was a seminal force in Elizabethan drama. He is the father of the revenge play, if not of English tragedy. His mastery of construction is unequaled before Shakespeare; and he may deserve some of the credit for introducing classical rhetoric and blank verse to the English stage. His *First Part of Hieronimo* and *The Spanish Tragedy*, especially the latter, were probably the most popular and influential of Elizabethan plays. They were performed, imitated, and parodied throughout the period; and even adapted in German and Dutch versions.[8] It is therefore specially important to reach a clearer

[3] See below, pp. xxxi–xxxii.
[4] Philip Edwards, ed., *The Spanish Tragedy* (*The Revels Plays*, London, 1959), p. xx.
[5] Boas, *Works*, p. lxiv.
[6] *Ibid.*, pp. lxvi ff.
[7] *Ibid.*, p. lxxvi.
[8] *Ibid.*, pp. xcix ff.

INTRODUCTION

understanding of these plays in their relation to each other and to a hypothetical *Ur-Hamlet*; and of their place, with relation to Marlowe and Shakespeare, in Elizabethan dramatic development.

The First Part of Hieronimo (or *Jeronimo*, as the name is often spelled in the old editions) was published in 1605. It was entered for copyright in the Stationers' Register by Thomas Pavier and published the same year with the title page:

> THE/ FIRST PART/ of Ieronimo./ With the Warres of Portugall, and the/ life and death of Don/ Andraea./ [device]/ Printed at London for Thomas Pauyer, and are/ to be solde at his shop, at the entrance/ into the Exchange 1605.[9]

The earliest extant and only authoritative text of *The Spanish Tragedy* is the edition—undated, but belonging to 1592—entitled:

> THE/ SPANISH TRAGE /die, Containing the lamentable/ end of *Don Horatio*, and *Bel-imperia*:/ with the pittifull death of/ olde *Hieronimo*./ Newly corrected and amended of such grosse faults as/ passed in the first impression./ [device]/ AT LONDON/ Printed by Edward Allde, for/ Edward White.[10]

The "first impression" presumably refers to an earlier edition, not extant, printed by Abell Jeffes, who entered it on the Stationers' Register on October 6, 1592:

> Abell Jeffes Entred for his copie vnder thandes of mr Hartwell and mr Stirrop, a booke w^che is called the Spanishe tragedie of Don Horatio and Bellimpera &c.

For, on December 18, 1592, a full court of the Stationers' Company ruled that White had offended "in publishing the spanish tragedie belonging to Abell Ieffes"; he was fined ten shillings and the edition was confiscated. The disputants seem, however, to have reached some agreement, since the next edition (1594) was "Printed by Abell Ieffes, and are to be sold by Edward White." These facts would be explained if Jeffes had entered and printed a defective text (thus acquiring the copyright); and if White had a good manuscript, which he used to correct and amend that of Jeffes. The 1594 compromise would thus combine the advantages of copyright and good text.

---
[9] It is perhaps worth noting that Q4 (1602), containing the "Additions," and Q5, of *The Spanish Tragedy*, were also published by Pavier.
[10] The sole extant copy is in the British Museum (C.34.d.7).

—xiii—

INTRODUCTION

The fourth quarto edition, 1602, was "Newly corrected, amended, and enlarged with new Additions of the *Painters* part and others."

The relation of *The Spanish Tragedy* to *The First Part of Hieronimo* is a major problem. Two contradictory solutions have been offered. Earlier views favored a two-part play by Kyd. Typical of such views was that of Sidney Lee, who found adequate internal evidence for assigning both plays to the same pen,[11] and that of Hartley Coleridge,[12] who called *1 Hieronimo* "the previous play." The extension in ink of the title of the British Museum copy of *The First Part of Hieronimo*, "or of the Spanish Tragedy," and the subtitle on the title page of the 1615 quarto of *The Spanish Tragedy*, "or Hieronimo is mad againe," would seem to support such opinions. Since Fischer[13] and Boas,[14] however, it has been accepted that *1 Hieronimo* is a later crude attempt, by some hack writer, to make capital out of the popularity of *The Spanish Tragedy*. In favor of this view, Boas urges the brevity and corruption of the text, and inconsistencies of plot and character. In the last half-century, however, we have had the revolution in the study of Elizabethan texts caused by the "memorial" theory of corrupt quartos like *1 Hieronimo*; and, if we assume that this is a memorial version of an original first part by Kyd, we may now return to a modified form of the earlier view.

There are certain obvious factors in favor of this return to the two-part play theory. Among the chief are the entries in Henslowe's *Diary*[15] that establish the existence of a fore-piece to *The Spanish Tragedy*. Between February 23 and June 20, 1592, Henslowe records thirteen performances by the combined Strange-Admiral's Company of a play called, in various spellings, *Hieronimo*. This Boas identifies, justifiably, with *The Spanish Tragedy*. The same play is later recorded, with the Admiral's Company alone, between December 30, 1593, and January 23, 1594,[16] and again in 1597;[17] and, under the same title, as the play for which Ben Jonson wrote "Additions" in 1601 and 1602.[18]

[11] *Dictionary of National Biography*, Vol. XXXI, p. 349, s.v. Kyd.
[12] Coleridge, *Table Talk* (London, 1884), p. 203.
[13] Rudolf Fischer, *Zur Kunstentwicklung der Englischen Tragödie* (Strassburg, 1893).
[14] Boas, *Works*, Introduction, pp. xxxix–xliv.
[15] *Henslowe's Diary*, ed. W. W. Greg (London, 1904), I, 13–15.
[16] *Ibid.*, p. 15.
[17] *Ibid.*, pp. 50–54.
[18] *Ibid.*, pp. 149, 168.

INTRODUCTION

In the same list of performances, Henslowe enters various other titles:

spanes comodye donne oracoe	1
the comodey of doneoracio	1
doneoracio	1
the comodey of Jeronymo	3
the comodey Jeronymo	1

We may assume, from knowledge of Henslowe's erratic spellings and the titles, that these refer to one and the same play. Now on five occasions a performance of *Hieronimo* (*The Spanish Tragedy*) was immediately or very closely preceded by a performance of the Don Horatio comedy (March 13, 14, 30, 31; April 10, 14, 22, 24; May 21, 22). It was, and is, therefore, natural to consider the comedy of *Hieronimo* (or *The Spanish Comedy*, or *The Comedy of Don Horatio*), and the tragedy of *Hieronimo* (or *The Tragedy of Don Horatio*, or *The Spanish Tragedy*) as a two-part play.

THE FIRST PART OF HIERONIMO

This view of *1 Hieronimo* can best be supported by noting the curious contradiction between the skilled, complicated construction and occasional strength of expression and characterization, on the one hand, and the many irregularities and defects of the play, on the other. Boas's theory was so colored by the obvious defects that he could see none of the virtues, even when they were clearly paralleled in *The Spanish Tragedy*. The contradiction does exist, however, and is incompatible with the idea of an original work, whether by competent dramatist or hack writer; but it can be simply explained by imperfect reporting or memorial reproduction of a competent original play by Kyd.

The text is indeed extremely corrupt. It is only some 1200 lines long.[19] Even in the absence of a good text for comparison, it seems clear that it is "memorial." The verse is most irregular and defective; but many lines may be simply mended by the omission of standard memorial particles and phrases, e.g.:

> What, doth it not promise fair?
> KING.
> Ay, and no doubt his merit will purchase more.
> Knight Marshal, rise, and still rise
> Higher and greater in thy sovereign's eyes. (i.18–21)

[19] Against *The Spanish Tragedy's* 2736 lines, without the "Additions."

Introduction

Here the particle "What" is metrically intrusive, as is probably also the vocative "Knight Marshal." The passage may therefore have read originally:

> Doth it not promise fair?
> KING.   Ay, and no doubt
> His merit will purchase more; rise, and still rise
> Higher and greater in thy sovereign's eyes.

Similarly, at i.27 (see textual note):

> The merry year, the peaceful year, jocund year,

may be regularised (as in the present edition) by treating the second "year" as a memorial repetition.

Disarrangement of material, another standard feature of memorial versions, may be seen at i.97–100:

> LORENZO.
>   Andrea's gone ambassador;
>   Lorenzo is not dreamt on in this age;
>   Hard fate,
>   When villains sit not in the highest state.

Here the first line could be transferred to the beginning of the third. It has probably also been repeated memorially at iii.36 and v.6, both spoken likewise by Lorenzo and both preceded by "Thou knowest/ You know."[20]

The style of *1 Hieronimo* is similarly irregular. But Schick[21] was able to point, in this play and in *The Spanish Tragedy*, to "stylistic resemblances in tropes and figures, parallel passages, ridiculous puns, common geographical mistakes," etc. And, allowing for imperfect reporting, the style of *1 Hieronimo* comes through clearly enough as that of *The Spanish Tragedy*, e.g.:

> I have a lad in pickle of this stamp,
> A melancholy, discontented courtier,
> Whose famish'd jaws look like the chap of death;
> Upon whose eyebrows hangs damnation; (i.113–116)

or

> My soul's a Moor, you know, salvation's white. (iii.61)

[20] Cf. also i.64–65 with i.80–81 for memorial duplication.
[21] J. Schick, ed., *The Spanish Tragedy* (London, 1898), p. xviii.

INTRODUCTION

Schick also pointed to the appearance in both plays of the same motifs and the same situations. Who but Kyd could have invented such a close parallel to the "intricate plot" of *The Spanish Tragedy*, with its "involved romantic intrigue"?[22] The rivalry of Andrea and Lorenzo, the overhearing of the plot by Hieronimo and Horatio, their warning letter to Andrea, possibly suspected by Lorenzo, the Alcario disguise, the crossing of the two plots in the shooting of Alcario in mistake for Andrea, the entry of Andrea at the critical moment, Lorenzo's silencing of Lazarotto just in time, the love-war encounter of Andrea and Bel-imperia, and the seeds of future conflict in (*a*) Andrea's dishonorable death, (*b*) Lorenzo's choice of Balthazar for Bel-imperia, and (*c*) the simultaneous disputed capture of Balthazar by Horatio and Lorenzo—stated thus, the elements of conflict, suspense, and romantic intrigue are here as in *The Spanish Tragedy*.[23]

In the light of the memorial theory, the very inconsistencies on which Boas relies for support of his view of *1 Hieronimo* tell against him. A hack writer using the material of *The Spanish Tragedy* was likely to produce a version of a fore-piece consistent with it; a memorial version by one or more actors, on the other hand, was likely to show gaps and inconsistencies, as in recognized Elizabethan bad quartos. If, for example, the reporting actor were not on stage during certain scenes, his report could leave considerable gaps. Further, if the original first part had been abridged, as Elizabethan plays often were,[24] for provincial performance, these gaps and inconsistencies are likely to have been increased. Thus it need not surprise us that *1 Hieronimo* contains nothing of certain previous events alluded to in *The Spanish Tragedy*, and is indeed incompatible with them. Boas[25] takes special note of the secret love of Andrea and Bel-imperia, and Castile's consequent "old wrath"; and of the fact that there is no sign of either secrecy or wrath in *1 Hieronimo*. That the "wrath" is a matter of omission is suggested by Castile's appearing only twice in the whole play—in scene i, with three words, and in scene viii, with none. The "secrecy" may be a matter of interpretation—secret

[22] Willard Farnham, *The Medieval Heritage of Elizabethan Tragedy* (Berkeley, 1936), pp. 391-392.
[23] Cf. also pp. xxix-xxx, below.
[24] See W. W. Greg, *Two Elizabethan Stage Abridgements: The Battle of Alcazar & Orlando Furioso* (Oxford, 1922).
[25] *Works*, p. xlii.

INTRODUCTION

from whom? Andrea's Ghost, in *The Spanish Tragedy* (I.i.10), says: "In secret I possess'd a worthy dame." Was it the "possession," not the whole affair, that was secret? These are just such gaps and inconsistencies as one might expect in a defective report.

There is a further inconsistency between the plays in their accounts of Andrea's death and the dishonor that justified the Ghost's desire for revenge.[26] *The Spanish Tragedy* gives a full account. Horatio relates how Nemesis

> Brought in a fresh supply of halberdiers,
> Which paunch'd his horse and ding'd him to the ground.
> Then young Don Balthazar with ruthless rage,
> Taking advantage of his foe's distress,
> Did finish what his halberdiers begun,
> And left not till Andrea's life was done.   (I.iv.21–26)

On which Bel-imperia comments:

> For what was't else but murderous cowardice,
> So many to oppress one valiant knight,
> Without respect of honor in the fight?   (I.iv.73–75)

Andrea was dishonorably overwhelmed by numbers instead of man-to-man in fair fight; Balthazar "took advantage" to kill him; and the whole was "murderous cowardice."

In *1 Hieronimo*, Andrea's death is represented thus:

> *They fight and* Andrea *hath* Balthazar *down. Enter* Portugales *and relieve* Balthazar *and kill* Andrea.
> ANDREA.
>   Oh, I am slain; help me, Horatio!
>   My foes are base, and slay me cowardly...   (xi.106.1–108)

The "author" of *1 Hieronimo* does not mention the horse; the halberdiers become merely "Portugales," and instead of Balthazar finishing "what his halberdiers begun," it is they who finish the work. A subsequent hack writer might have been expected to make a fuller and more accurate reproduction of the information at his disposal in *The Spanish Tragedy*. But the reporter of an old original first part might easily be thus inaccurate, remembering only such key-words as "base" and "cowardly." The inadequacy and inconsistency, in short, favor a memorial version.

[26] He was not "slain in fair fight," as Boas (*Works*, p. xxxiii) claims.

INTRODUCTION

The same line of argument may be applied to other discrepancies between the two plays—of character, generally more apparent than real, which may be ascribed to change of circumstance, or corruption in the text, in *1 Hieronimo*; and of plot, where again inconsistency[27] is more probable in a memorial version than in a later hack writer's attempt.

Finally, because of Henslowe's term "comedy," Boas[28] was led to speak of the "forepiece" as "humorous." A comedy, however, is not necessarily humorous or comic. All that is required is that it should end happily, like Dante's *Divine Comedy*. And *1 Hieronimo*, in spite of the death of Andrea—like the *Divine Comedy* in spite of the *Inferno*—ends happily. Andrea's is a "happy ghost" (xii.19) and "rejoices" (xii.8, 16):

> The day is ours and joy yields happy treasure;
> Set on to Spain in most triumphant measure.   (xiii.5–6)

It therefore seems reasonable to suggest as the original of which *1 Hieronimo* is a memorial version a longer good text by Kyd, *The Spanish Comedy*, which preceded *The Spanish Tragedy* and combined with it to form a two-part play.

THE SPANISH TRAGEDY

The text of *The Spanish Tragedy*, though much superior to that of *1 Hieronimo*, is not itself free from suspicion, especially from III.xv on. No doubt there has been an element of revision. The play in "unknown languages," for example, promised at IV.i.168–174,[29] is given in English, with the prefatory note:

> *Gentlemen, this play of* Hieronimo, *in sundry languages, was thought good to be set down in English, more largely, for the easier understanding to every public reader.*   (IV.iv.10.2–4)

It has been suggested that this English version is the original, which was later cut to a mime, with some gibberish, and that the reference to unknown languages was an insertion at the same time. This would agree with "more largely," and with the fact that an outline of the plot has already been given, at IV.i.106–128. Similarly, it may be a

---

[27] E.g., the reappearance of Don Pedro in *The Spanish Tragedy* after he has been killed in *1 Hieronimo*. Was this due to confusion with Pedringano, or to doubling? See Boas, *Works*, p. xliv, footnote.
[28] *Works*, p. xli.
[29] Cf. IV.iv.74–75.

INTRODUCTION

mark of revision that Hieronimo, at the end of the play-scene, has no justification for not revealing something he has in fact told already, at IV.iv.83–152.[30]

Revision, however, will not explain the corruption of III.xv; the metrical irregularity common elsewhere (cf. IV.i.48 ff.); the superfluous stage directions *Enter* and *Exeunt* for the Ghost and Revenge, who remain as spectators throughout; the curious "*Then he makes signs for a knife to mend his pen*" (IV.iv.197.1), which may be derived from the text (l. 198); and such peculiar features as the duplicate stage directions at II.ii.6.1–2 and 17.1, and III.i.0.1 (see textual note) and 30.1, which parallel the inconsistency of IV.iv.208: "And thou, Don Pedro, [bear the body]," with the stage direction at 216.2: "*the* King . . . *bearing the body*."

Nor will revision explain a number of what must be memorial phrases, e.g.:

LORENZO.
    I'll trust myself, myself shall be my friend;
    For die they shall, slaves are ordained to no other end.
                  III.ii.118–119 (see textual note)

Here the italicized phrase is hypermetrical and an "anticipation" of III.iv.37 (a scene in which Lorenzo is also present):

    For die he shall for this his damned deed.[31]

There also occur many of the intrusive particles so familiar in memorial texts,[32] and not likely to be due to compositor or editor. There is even some metrical irregularity in the first half of the play. In the rest the corruption occurs in patches, the worst being III.ii.56 ff., IV.i.48 onwards, and IV.iii. This irregularity in itself seems to confirm the use, where thought convenient, of memorial copy. In two places (IV.i.56, 152), moreover, repetition and defective meter concur to suggest the intrusion of actors' cues, often found in bad texts. In short, the play, and especially the second half, shows all the features of a text that has had occasional recourse to memorial copy.

Edwards suggests the probable explanation—the use of Jeffes's lost memorial edition, collated with certain parts of the authentic

---

[30] Cf. Edwards, pp. xxxiv–xxxvi.
[31] Cf. Lorenzo's "For die he must, if we do mean to live" (III.ii.86).
[32] See textual notes on III.ii.58, "(up)on"; III.iv.30, "to"; III.viii.10, "Why"; and, for other probable intrusions, III.ii.57 and 60, "Hieronimo"; III.ix.15, "Madam"; III.xiv.46, "Who"; and III.xiv.149, "good."

INTRODUCTION

manuscript to provide printer's copy. Such memorial or bad texts were clearly employed in this way for the printing of the good quarto texts of *Romeo and Juliet* and *Hamlet*, and the Folio texts of *Henry V*, *2* and *3 Henry VI* and *Richard III*. If *The Spanish Tragedy* was printed in this manner, the reason was more likely to have been a desire for speed and convenience in the printing-house than a defective manuscript.[33]

THE ADDITIONS OF 1602

Thomas Pavier's edition of 1602 added to the text of *The Spanish Tragedy* five passages totaling over three hundred lines. These have sometimes been ascribed to Ben Jonson, on the strength of two entries in Henslowe's *Diary*:[34]

Lent vnto m^r alleyn the 25 of september/ 1601 to lend vnto Bengemen Johnson vpon/ his writtinge of his adicians in geronymo/ the some of } xxxx^s

Lent vnto bengemy Johnsone at the poyntment of E Alleyn/ and w^m birde the 22 of June 1602/ in earneste of a Boocke called Richard/ crockbacke & for new adicyons for/ Jeronymo the some of } x^{li}

The "additions" may indeed be Jonson's; but there has been almost universal objection to his authorship. It has been argued that the amount, even allowing for the "Crookback" play, paid for some three hundred lines, is excessive. Again, such additions were "unlikely to reach the press so soon," and Pavier was more likely "to pass off old matter as new than to secure the latest theatrical novelty."[35]

Further, the Painter scene is parodied by Marston in the earlier *Antonio and Mellida*, and in the third Addition in *Antonio's Revenge*.[36] Both plays are generally dated 1599, or at the latest 1600.[37] To meet

[33] See Edwards, pp. xxxviii–xl.
[34] I, 149, 168.
[35] *The Spanish Tragedy with Additions 1602*. The Malone Society Reprints, 1925 (Oxford), p. xix.
[36] Edwards, Appendix E.
[37] E. K. Chambers, *The Elizabethan Stage* (Oxford, 1923), III, 429–430; H. Levin, "An echo from *The Spanish Tragedy*," *Modern Language Notes*, LXIV (1949), 297–302. Cf. G. K. Hunter, ed., *Antonio and Mellida* (Regents Renaissance Drama Series, Lincoln, 1965), pp. ix–x.

INTRODUCTION

these objections, it has been suggested that the additions belong to 1597, when the play was revived, marked "ne" (new?), by the Admiral's Men.[38] This would certainly give time for the parodies by Marston; and it would also lend meaning to the reference, in Jonson's *Cynthia's Revels*[39] (written about 1600) to a lapse of "a dozen yeeres" since "*the old Hieronimo*, (as it was first acted)." The last phrase could then be read as an indirect allusion to additions of 1597, as distinct from the original old play.[40]

The main objection to Jonson's authorship, however, whether of 1602 or 1597, is the internal evidence of style. Herford and Simpson, for example, remark that Henslowe's entries "cannot guarantee, if there is strong internal evidence to the contrary, that the work undertaken by Jonson was not carried out by some one else."[41] "There is nothing," says Charles Lamb, "in the undoubted plays of Jonson which would authorize us to suppose that he could have supplied the scenes in question. I should suspect the agency of some 'more potent spirit'."[42] Various potent spirits have indeed been suggested, such as Webster (Lamb),[43] Shakespeare (Coleridge),[44] and even Dekker.[45] But there is, in fact, no Elizabethan dramatist who wrote quite in this style.

It may be worth speculating on the alternative possibility that the "additions" are not additions at all, but original passages cut and later restored to the text, and written by Kyd himself. Here again, probably, few would agree that the style is Kyd's. It lacks his numerous rhetorical devices and figures. On the other hand, his style is adaptable to the matter and situation; and the Painter addition at least is not so unlike the corresponding original scene.

All five additions are devoted to the elaboration of a single theme—"the harrowing grief of Hieronimo for his son";[46] and represent

[38] *Henslowe's Diary*, I, 50, 223.
[39] *Ben Jonson*, ed. C. H. Herford and Percy Simpson (Oxford, 1925–1942), IV, 41–42.
[40] *The Spanish Tragedy (1592)*. The Malone Society Reprints, 1948(1949), (Oxford University Press), pp. xiv–xv.
[41] *Jonson*, II, 245.
[42] Charles Lamb, *Specimens of English Dramatic Poets* (London, 1854), p. 11, footnote.
[43] *Ibid*.
[44] *Table Talk*, p. 210.
[45] H. W. Crundell and R. G. Howarth, *Notes and Queries*, March 4, 1933; April 7, August 4, 1934; January 4, 1941.
[46] *Jonson*, II, 239.

INTRODUCTION

transitions between the mad and the sane Hieronimo—that is, they are of poetic and psychological rather than dramatic value. They contribute little or nothing to the plot of an already long play. Abbreviation, rather than addition, would be in keeping with the length of the play, and serve to reduce the heavy part of Hieronimo; and the nature of the passages makes them peculiarly liable to cutting, with gain rather than loss to the plot and dramatic tempo.

Schücking's suggestion[47] that the "additions" were in fact replacements—"duplications" would be still better—comes nearest to this theory, and applies exactly to part of the Painter scene. This "addition" treats of precisely the same theme—justice for a murdered son—as III.xiii.67–175, but more briefly. The two scenes, however, may be supplementary; the "addition" ends—III.xiiA.(*161.1*)— with the same stage direction (*with a book in his hand*) as that which begins the original scene (III.xiii.0.1). Part of the "addition" could therefore be an alternative to part of the original text; or again, like the rest, it might be original and cut.

The remaining four "additions" are not susceptible of this "alternative" explanation. They belong. The "seams" are agreed to be on the whole neat—too neat for additions. The third, admittedly, seems to break the continuity between III.xi.1, "By your leave, sir" and III.xi.2, "Good leave have you." But it could be equally well explained as a felicitous excision of a madman's digression which he must elaborate before returning to the request he has for the moment thrust aside—a digression which by its nature invites cutting.

The subject matter of the "additions" is remarkably consistent. The fourth discusses justice for a son; the third deals with the nature of a son. The first is a neat psychological unit describing an initial temporary mental aberration of Hieronimo, who has "lost my way to grief" for his son, and his return to reality. The second seems too short to have been worth while adding. The fifth merely expresses general sentiments which the lines preserved from the earlier version cover adequately.

The problem is further complicated by the textual condition of the "additions." They share the corruption of the main text; which in turn suggests that, though delayed in publication, they underwent the same process of transmission. Besides metrical defects, too great and too numerous for a compositor, there are intrusive memorial

[47] Edwards, pp. lxiii–lxiv; L. L. Schücking, *Die Zusätze zur "Spanish Tragedy"* (Leipzig, 1938).

phrases and particles. The fourth "addition," for example, seems to illustrate a reporter's trick of repetition:[48]

> Not I, indeed; we are *very* merry, very merry.   (III.xiiA.[*58*])
> It bore thy fruit and mine—oh *wicked*, wicked plant!   [*71*][49]
>   (see textual notes)

This corruption presents a dilemma. If the "additions" are Jonson's, there is no problem as to the expansions, omissions, and rearrangements of the text. But why then is it still corrupt? Is this also a report, and if so, by whom? How did Pavier obtain it? If, on the other hand, the "additions" really restore cuts or alternatives, by what process of conflation do parts of the fifth "addition," for example, survive in two different versions, with reversal of order, corrections—e.g. IV.iv.182, (*197*)—and omissions? And if the "additions" are not Jonson's, what happened to those he was paid for in 1601 and 1602? The problem remains baffling.

CRITICAL

THEME

The Spanish Tragedy suffers to some extent from being a sequel. It has to recapitulate much that has already been presented in *1 Hieronimo*. Not only has the Induction to explain the previous action to Revenge and the audience, but the explanation has to be repeated at length (I.iv) for Bel-imperia. The first act thus tends to move slowly; narration hinders the dramatic momentum. This is probably the price paid for a technique in which a play is at once a dependent sequel and yet may be acted and seen independently. The technique may be seen again, for example, in Shakespeare's *3 Henry VI* and *Richard III*. Even if *The Spanish Tragedy* had been written alone, before *1 Hieronimo*, its assumption and recapitulation of so much previous material would still present a difficult technical problem, especially in a play of such rapid and exciting action.

In both plays the emphasis falls on incident, structure, and suspense more than on character. Both are marked by "intricate plot, with devious scheming," and "involved romantic intrigue," in which

---

[48] Cf. *1 Hieronimo*, i.27.
[49] Cf. *1 Hieronimo*, ii.4: "That's Bel-imperia./ See, *see*, she meets you here": and ii.28: ". . . both . . . *both* . . ." (see textual note).

INTRODUCTION

there is "an instinctive discrimination for utilizing incident melodramatically and for making his [Kyd's] story into 'good theatre'".[50] *1 Hieronimo* suffers somewhat from its corruption and the consequent blurring of outline, and from minor inconsistencies, but the general plan is clear enough. The love intrigue in both plays centers on Bel-imperia, in her successive relations with Don Andrea and Don Horatio, and the opposition of her family. The opposition comes from her father Castile and her brother Lorenzo, who plots to kill Andrea and Horatio in favor of their rivals Alcario and Balthazar. In each play, Lorenzo successfully disposes of his agent, Lazarotto or Pedringano, promising a pardon. In each Hieronimo acts to counter crimes, and save or avenge the victim.

The two plays differ, of course, in general theme and tone. *1 Hieronimo* is the comedy of Spanish victory over Portugal, even at the cost of Andrea's life; *The Spanish Tragedy* is a complicated revenge tragedy.

1 Hieronimo is mainly concerned with a war, and the honor and dishonor involved in its conduct. The play begins with honor; Hieronimo is honored by his appointment as Marshal of Spain ("Age ushers honor" [i.30]), Andrea by his choice as ambassador to Portugal. Andrea is "poor, though honorable" (iii.49), "the heir of honor" (viii.43), a "noble rib of honor" (xi.149); he "aims at honor" (i.106). His honor ranks above the claims of love, and he must leave Bel-imperia (ii); he is received with honor by the Portuguese, especially by his counterpart, Don Balthazar, and they look forward with eagerness to honorable conflict. Bel-imperia is afraid he will "lean much to honor" (ii.20) and prove too rigidly honorable for his diplomatic mission. On his death he is given "honor'd rites" by the Spaniards, particularly his honorable friend Horatio. Spain as a whole is dishonored by the denial of Portugal's tribute (ix.4), solemnly sworn to; Portugal by her subjection to Spain (iv.24); the Portuguese will resist and die with honor (x.12–21).

Confronting honor is policy, expressed in baseness, cowardice, ambition, pride, luxury, and the power of gold—all once predominant and still prevalent in courts (i.101–105; iii.24, 30–32; x.25–26). Policy is represented chiefly by Lorenzo and his tool Lazarotto, but is finally reinforced by the accession of the apparently honorable Balthazar, who with his men kills Andrea dishonorably.[51]

[50] Farnham, pp. 391–392.
[51] xi.108. This is the kernel of *The Spanish Tragedy*: see I.ii.65–72; I.iv.21–26, 73–76.

INTRODUCTION

In *The Spanish Tragedy* the opposition of honor and policy continues a main theme. The Viceroy of Portugal is received honorably in Spain. But now honor appears less and less in the courts. Villuppo accuses Alexandro falsely (I.iii) for gold and promotion (III.i.95); Pedringano kills Serberine for gold (III.iii); and the politic Lorenzo unscrupulously rids himself of Pedringano, as he did of Lazarotto. Balthazar, with the instigation and help of Lorenzo, decides to "tempt the Destinies" in his pursuit of Bel-imperia by various dishonorable means. The unjust have become more numerous and effective than the just, are more ingenious and unscrupulous and more favored by rank, wealth, and of course their lack of conscience. The just, on the other hand, have to wait and suffer in their maintenance of honor and their quest for justice. It is only by acquiring some of his enemies' ingenuity and fighting them with their own weapons that Hieronimo, in the event, can secure what justice there is; and then only at the cost of his own life and Bel-imperia's.

But the major enveloping theme is now revenge, represented by the Chorus. As in Shakespeare, one human revenge sets off another. The original dishonor, Andrea's death, which will be revenged through the action of the whole play, sets off Bel-imperia's quest for revenge on Balthazar. Her adoption of Horatio as the instrument sets off in turn the revenge of Lorenzo and Balthazar in the dishonorable murder of Horatio by hanging; which itself is the mainspring of Hieronimo's final comprehensive revenge, in which the wheel comes full circle, avenging Andrea as well as Horatio. Although this is ostensibly a human, not a divine revenge, it is in a sense raised to that level by the sanction of the Ghost, and the allocation, by whatever gods may be, of appropriate punishments in Hades for the offenders.

The theme of revenge raises that of justice, for revenge, as Bacon says, is a kind of wild justice. The theme is announced in the Induction, where Andrea's case "is decided, not by the judges of hell, who cannot agree; nor by their infernal King; but by Proserpina, who—for a smiling plea, sealed with a kiss—is allowed by her indulgent husband to decide Andrea's future and pronounce Balthazar's doom."[52] The decision, however, is not so much in question as the procedure. Mortal justice is represented by the Villuppo

[52] This, and the following points, slightly modified, I owe to a paper, "Taking Kyd seriously," read at the 1964 meeting of the Modern Language Association by Dr. Robert Hapgood, University of New Hampshire.

Introduction

incident in which the Viceroy of Portugal condemns Alexandro on "an envious, forged tale" without hearing his evidence. In Spain, Lorenzo uses his influence to thwart Hieronimo's appeal for justice. The king himself is too involved with international relations to take notice of the appeal, treats Balthazar as prospective bridegroom and heir rather than as a prisoner of war—thus undoing at one blow all that Andrea had died for—and apparently does nothing to bring justice on the murderers of Horatio. The result is that his leniency assists Balthazar's suit, which leads to Bel-imperia's preference for Horatio and his death, which is the occasion of Hieronimo's revenge.

It is, in fact, an unjust, dishonorable world, in which Hieronimo (with Isabella and Bel-imperia) is left alone to secure what justice he can for himself. He should have had it from the King; if not, then from heaven (or perhaps hell); but since neither seems effective, he is forced to take it into his own hands. At first, as an officer of the law, he is in favor of legal justice or the justice of the heavens. As Isabella says:

> The heavens are just; murder cannot be hid;
> Time is the author both of truth and right,
> And time will bring this treachery to light.
> (II.v.57–59)

Later, administering justice—"blood with blood" (III.vi.35)—to Pedringano, he has come to feel

> That only I to all men just must be,
> And neither gods nor men be just to me.
> (III.vi.9–10)

He has

> Beat at the windows of the brightest heavens,
> Soliciting for justice and revenge:
> (III.vii.13–14)

but finds "the place impregnable" (l. 17). On receiving Pedringano's letter, revealing the murderers, he decides to go to the King for justice (III.vii.69–70). Thanks to Lorenzo, and Hieronimo's own suspicions and incipient madness, there is no justice to be had there: and he suggests going instead to the Elysian plains, where he thinks Rhadamanth will oblige him. Meanwhile, on the failure of public or divine justice, there comes the passive reaction of Isabella's madness and suicide. After paying further lip-service to divine vengeance

INTRODUCTION

(III.xiii), Hieronimo abruptly decides to take revenge into his own hands in due time, since justice cannot be found on earth (III.xiii.108, 138–139).

Finally, with Bel-imperia's help, which he takes as a sign of divine approval (IV.i.31–33), Hieronimo plans the play which will do justice on all the offenders. There Lorenzo, Balthazar, and Castile are slain, and justice is done for the murders of Andrea and Horatio, as well as for the "old disgrace" of Bel-imperia in her affair with Andrea. Thereafter Andrea allocates just, if apparently excessive, rewards and punishments to the spirits of the dead.

It has been argued that this last act is "mere massacre ... a series of blood-curdling incidents.... And the note of sheer savagery is prolonged in the epilogue where Andrea's Ghost gloats over the prospect of his enemies suffering eternal torment in hell."[53] It is true, indeed, that the physical horrors of Hieronimo's revenge, like the Ghost's punishments, may seem excessive and repulsive. But they are not unjustified, nor is Kyd's dramatic instinct at fault. He is taking full account of the dishonorable deaths of Andrea and Horatio, Castile's opposition to Andrea's love-affair, the futile search for justice and the sufferings of Hieronimo and his family; he is saying, in effect, that these "enormities climax the unjust ways of the world ... depicted throughout."[54] The Senecan tongue-biting, for example, is more than a physical horror: it is a powerful symbol by which Hieronimo "registers his madness and pushes to an ultimate his self-defeating incapacity to express his cause to the king."[55] In his sufferings and reactions, Hieronimo has thus our full appreciation and sympathy, and the theme of the play is complete: justice has been done. It is tragic that it can be done only in this extreme bloodthirsty fashion; and that in its execution it has to involve the innocent with the guilty.

STRUCTURE

Outside of the main action, there are many subsidiary episodes, which at first sight seem irrelevant to the main theme of vengeance. But the Alexandro–Villuppo incident, as indicated above, forms part of the justice theme. That of Pedringano–Serberine does the same, and also leads back, through the letter device, to the revenge

[53] Boas, *Works*, p. xxxix.
[54] Hapgood, *op. cit.*
[55] *Ibid.*

INTRODUCTION

theme. The mime presented by Hieronimo (I.iv), and the dumb-show of revenge (III.xv), may seem extraneous: but in effect they perform several useful functions. They present simultaneously spectacle and melodrama, mixed with patriotism. They also illustrate Hieronimo's dramatic talent in preparing for the final play-scene, and foreshadow the catastrophe in store for Spain and Portugal.[56]

Both plays obviously depend much less on character than on plot, that is, on suspense. Who, in *1 Hieronimo*, is to be chosen ambassador to Portugal? Will Don Andrea be able to control his temper? Hieronimo and Horatio overhear Lorenzo's plan to murder Andrea: can they prevent it? Will Lorenzo discover the contents of Hieronimo's warning letter to Andrea? Will Lazarotto confess and betray Lorenzo? Which army and which of the leaders, Andrea or Balthazar, will win? The same technique, for example the last-minute reprieve of Alexandro, and, in reverse, of Pedringano, is obvious enough in *The Spanish Tragedy*. Many of these situations are accompanied, in both plays, by skilful use of irony, as in the box incident at Pedringano's hanging; and they are reinforced by such equivocation as Lorenzo's "Thou shalt mount for this" (to Pedringano), or Hieronimo's sustained irony while allocating the parts in his play.

In the same way, *The Spanish Tragedy* uses the necessary delay in revenge to create and maintain suspense. The question is "Who killed Horatio?" The situation evolves into a battle of wits, with Hieronimo trying to find out, Lorenzo to conceal, the truth. The conflict is drawn out by the discovery of Pedringano's and Bel-imperia's letters, and by Hieronimo's suspicion of a trap, Lorenzo's counter-action in preventing access to the King, the apparent reconciliation of Lorenzo and Hieronimo, and finally Hieronimo's play-device.

Horror and violence are in keeping with this melodramatic trend. The murders of Alcario and Horatio, the bloody letter and handkerchief, the tongue-biting, the ghosts, the hangings and corpses, the threats of torture, as well as the violent loves of Bel-imperia, and the use of the Virgilian underworld to begin and end *The Spanish Tragedy*—all these are typical of the melodramatic and Senecan foundations of the plays.

The characters are likewise typical of melodrama. The minor figures are slight and indeterminate. The central characters—the chivalrous Andrea and Horatio, the ingenious intriguing Lorenzo,

[56] I owe much of this paragraph to Dr. Harold Brooks.

INTRODUCTION

the proud inflexible Bel-imperia—are simple to excess. They are in a sense caricatures, evolving according to their given humors, more by illustrative incident than by internal development. All are strong, asserting their wills against the obstacles they meet. Hieronimo is more complicated, and there is considerable psychological insight in the progress of his mental disturbance, and his development from a symbol of honor and justice into the pattern of an unscrupulous avenger. The most indeterminate character is Balthazar, who is at first apparently honorable, but who reveals his truer nature in the fight with Andrea, and later, under the influence of Lorenzo, in his suit to Bel-imperia.

To a degree not yet fully analyzed,[57] Kyd's dialogue maintains decorum, reflecting the characters and their dramatic situation. There is considerable variation from verse to prose, from full-scale rhetorical speech to incisive brevity and staccato dialogue. All the figures of classical rhetoric are at his command.[58] The effect, as with the portrayal of character, is in general rather artificial; but the technical skill is as evident as in the handling of plot and incident.

DATE

The limits of date are set by (*a*) Kyd's use of Thomas Watson's *Hecatompathia* (Stationers' Register, March 3, 1582),[59] and (*b*) Henslowe's entries of February 23 and March 14, 1592.[60] The downward limit may be narrowed to 1590–1591 by Shakespeare's use of *Spanish Tragedy* material in *3 Henry VI*.[61] The interval accords roughly with Jonson's allusion in the Induction to *Bartholomew Fair* (1614); "Hee that will sweare, *Ieronimo*, or *Andronicus* are the best playes, yet, shall passe vnexcepted at, heere, as a man whose Iudgement shewes it is constant, and hath stood still, these fiue and twentie, or thirtie yeeres".[62] This gives the period from 1584 to 1589; and, though Jonson is obviously using round figures, the inclusion of *Titus Andronicus* tends to corroborate the limits he suggests.

[57] But see W. Clemen, *Die Tragödie vor Shakespeare* (Heidelberg, 1955).
[58] Cf. F. G. Hubbard, "Repetition and Parallelism in the Earlier Elizabethan Drama," *Publications of the Modern Language Association*, XX (1905), 360–379.
[59] See *The Spanish Tragedy*, II.i.2–10, note.
[60] See above, pp. xiv–xv.
[61] *3 Henry VI*, I.iv.79–82; 156–163.
[62] *Jonson*, VI, 16.

—xxx—

INTRODUCTION

Further grounds for the date of the Spanish plays are: (*a*) Kyd's letter to Puckering,[63] which would push the later limit back to 1587; (*b*) Nashe's attack of 1589. These, and others, while not amounting to certainty, converge on the probability that the plays were written about 1585–1587. Nashe writes as follows:

> It is a common practise now a dayes amongst a sort of shifting companions, that runne through euery Art and thriue by none, to leaue the trade of *Nouerint*, whereto they were borne, and busie themselues with the indeuours of Art, that could scarcely Latinize their neck verse if they should haue neede; yet English *Seneca* read by Candle-light yeelds many good sentences, as *Blood is a begger*, and so forth; and if you intreate him faire in a frostie morning, hee will affoord you whole Hamlets, I should say handfuls of Tragicall speeches. But O griefe! *Tempus edax rerum*, whats that will last alwayes? The Sea exhaled by droppes will in continuance bee drie, and *Seneca*, let blood line by line and page by page, at length must needes die to our Stage; which makes his famished followers to imitate the Kid in *Æsop*, who, enamoured with the Foxes newfangles, forsooke all hopes of life to leape into a new occupation; and these men, renouncing all possibilities of credite or estimation, to intermeddle with Italian Translations: Wherein how poorely they haue plodded, (as those that are neither prouenzall men, nor are able to distinguish of Articles,) let all indifferent Gentlemen that haue trauelled in that tongue discerne by their two-pennie Pamphlets. And no maruell though their home borne mediocritie bee such in this matter; for what can bee hoped of those that thrust *Elisium* into hell, and haue not learned, so long as they haue liued in the Spheres, the iust measure of the Horizon without an hexameter? Sufficeth them to bodge vp a blanke verse with ifs and ands....[64]

Out of the dust of controversy,[65] it would now seem to emerge that (*a*) Nashe was attacking more than one writer ("a sort of ... these men"), (*b*) one of whom was Kyd ("the Kid in *Æsop*"), the imitator

[63] See above, pp. xi–xii.
[64] "To the Gentlemen Students," prefaced to Greene's *Menaphon,* 1589, in R. B. McKerrow, ed., *The Works of Thomas Nashe* (Oxford, 1904–1910: reprint of 1958), III, 315–316.
[65] See, e.g., Boas, *Works*, pp. xlv–liv; McKerrow, *Nashe*, IV, 449–452; G. I. Duthie, *The Bad Quarto of "Hamlet"* (Cambridge, 1941), pp. 55–78.

INTRODUCTION

of Seneca, the author of Italian translations, and the son of a scrivener, or noverint-maker.

The *Hamlet* reference raises a more complicated and difficult point. Boas, noting the many close parallels in plot and phrase with *The Spanish Tragedy*, unaware of the "memorial" nature of the First Quarto of *Hamlet*, and not even considering that Shakespeare could have written plays as early as 1589, assumed an *Ur-Hamlet*, by Kyd, as the foundation on which Shakespeare later built his play. The parallels,[66] however, are better interpreted as quotation, imitation, or reporting than as self-repetition; and Shakespeare is at least as likely to have written *Hamlet* (whatever version) then.[67] If so, this helps to put *The Spanish Tragedy* back to at least 1587, to allow for such a deep impression and such a complex imitation. Nashe's attack would further link with his friend Greene's later invective (1592) on Shakespeare as the "Iohannes factotum" who thought himself "the onely Shake-scene in a countrey" and who could "bombast out" a blank verse with sentences and "tragicall speeches" from Seneca—Seneca who had (in Kyd) been "let blood" and would soon (in Shakespeare) "die to our stage."

Professor Fredson Bowers,[68] who accepted an *Ur-Hamlet* and who regards the first quarto text of *Hamlet* as a form of it,[69] would date *The Spanish Tragedy* as late as 1590, *after* the *Ur-Hamlet*, on the ground that the themes of madness and delay are in Belleforest (a direct source of *Hamlet*), and therefore secondary in *The Spanish Tragedy*. But delay is necessary in any play of some length; and Hieronimo's madness is real enough (not feigned like Hamlet's), a natural result of his frustration in pursuit of justice; behind it is a long literary tradition. Naturally, Bowers finds it curious that Kyd should then (in *The Spanish Tragedy*) "abstract the two best dramatic features to create an original plot instead of dramatizing Belleforest's story where they were native."[70] He does not mention, either, the actual borrowings in *Hamlet* from *The Spanish Tragedy*,[71] nor the lack of "adequate psychological analysis of the Marshal's motives for this delay,"[72]

[66] Boas, *Works*, pp. l–li.
[67] Alexander, p. 197. Henslowe (I, 17) records a performance of *Hamlet* on June 9, 1594.
[68] *Elizabethan Revenge Tragedy* (Princeton, 1940), p. 96.
[69] *Ibid.*, p. 86.
[70] *Ibid.*, p. 96.
[71] *Hamlet*, III.ii.304–305 ("For if . . . perdy").
[72] Boas, *Works*, p. xxxv.

INTRODUCTION

as contrasted with the profound analysis of *Hamlet*. It would seem more natural, therefore, to have the order of the plays the other way round.

Other evidence for the dates of these plays of Kyd is inconclusive, especially that of borrowings, echoes, and parallels. It has been suggested, for example,[73] that Kyd borrowed from Watson's *Meliboeus* (1590), a free English rendering of his own Latin version. It is equally probable, however, that the very slight and commonplace parallels, if really more than fortuitous, show influence in the other direction.

In general, then, the evidence seems to favor a date for the Spanish plays between 1585 and 1587.

ANDREW S. CAIRNCROSS

Texas Technological College

[73] Edwards, Appendix D.

THE FIRST PART OF HIERONIMO

[DRAMATIS PERSONAE

King of Spain
Duke of Castile, *his brother*
Lorenzo, *the Duke's son*
Bel-imperia, *Lorenzo's sister*
Pedringano, *Bel-imperia's servant*

King of Portugal
Don Pedro, *his brother*
Balthazar, *the King's son*

Hieronimo, *Marshal of Spain*
Isabella, *his wife*
Horatio, *their son*

Duke Medina
Alcario, *his son*
Andrea
Rogero } *Spanish courtiers*
Lazarotto
Spanish Ambassador
Spanish Lord General
Spanish Captain
Portuguese Lord General
Villuppo } *Portuguese noblemen*
Alexandro
Messenger

Ghost of Andrea
Revenge
Charon

Nobles, Soldiers, Attendants, Mourners]

[Dramatis Personae] *from Boas.*

[The Spanish Comedy

or]

The First Part of Hieronimo

[i]

Sound a sennet, and pass over the stage. Enter at one door the King of Spain, Duke of Castile, Duke Medina, Lorenzo, *and* Rogero: *at another door,* Andrea, Horatio, *and* Hieronimo. Hieronimo *kneels down, and the* King *creates him Marshal of Spain:* Lorenzo *puts on his spurs, and* Andrea *his sword. The* King *goes along with* Hieronimo *to his house. After a long sennet is sounded, enter all the nobles, with cover'd dishes, to the banquet. Exeunt omnes. That done, enter all again as before.*

KING.
    Frolic, Hieronimo; thou art now confirm'd
    Marshal of Spain, by all the due
    And customary rites unto thy office.
HIERONIMO.
    My knee signs thanks unto your highness' bounty;
    Come hither, boy Horatio; fold thy joints;   5
    Kneel by thy father's loins, and thank my liege
    For honoring me, thy mother, and thy self
    With this high staff of office.
HORATIO.   Oh my liege,
    I have a heart thrice stronger than my years,
    And that shall answer gratefully for me.   10

2. due] *B*; dewes *Q*.   sings *Q, edd*.
4. signs] *this edn., conj. Brereton;*   7. For] *B;* by *Q*.

0.1. *sennet*] flourish on trumpet or cornet, indicating a royal entry or exit.

The First Part of Hieronimo

Let not my youthful blush impair my valor:
If ever you have foes, or red field scars,
I'll empty all my veins to serve your wars:
I'll bleed for you; and more, what speech affords,
I'll speak in drops, when I do fail in words. 15

HIERONIMO.
Well spoke, my boy; and on thy father's side.
My liege, how like you Don Horatio's spirit?
What, doth it not promise fair?

KING.
Ay, and no doubt his merit will purchase more.
Knight Marshal, rise, and still rise 20
Higher and greater in thy sovereign's eyes.

HIERONIMO.
Oh fortunate hour, blessed minute, happy day,
Able to ravish even my sense away.
Now I remember too—oh sweet remembrance!—
This day my years strike fifty, and in Rome 25
They call the fifty year the year of Jubilee,
The merry year, the peaceful, jocund year,
A year of joy, of pleasure, and delight.
This shall be my year of Jubilee, for 'tis my fifty.
Age ushers honor; 'tis no shame; confess, 30
Beard, thou art fifty full, not a hair less.

Enter an Ambassador.

KING.
How now, what news for Spain? tribute return'd?

AMBASSADOR.
Tribute in words, my liege, but not in coin.

KING.
Ha! dare he still procrastinate with Spain?
Not tribute paid, not three years paid? 35
'Tis not at his coin,

18. What, doth] *Q;* Doth *conj. this edn.* peaceful yeere *Q;* peaceful yeere, the *Hz.*
27. peaceful] *this edn., conj.* Brereton; 32. for] *C, Hz, B;* from *Q.*

---

11. *impair*] discredit.
26. *Jubilee*] See Leviticus 25.

-4-

But his slack homage, that we most repine.

HIERONIMO.
My liege, if my opinion might stand firm
Within you highness' thoughts—

KING.
Marshal, our kingdom calls thee father: 40
Therefore speak free.
Thy counsel I'll embrace as I do thee.

HIERONIMO.
I thank your highness. Then, my gracious liege,
I hold it meet, by way of embassage,
To demand his mind and the neglect of tribute. 45
But, my liege,
Here must be kind words which doth oft besiege
The ears of rough-hewn tyrants more than blows:
Oh, a politic speech beguiles the ears of foes.
Marry, my liege, mistake me not, I pray; 50
If friendly phrases, honey'd speech, bewitching accent,
Well-tuned melody, and all sweet gifts of nature,
Cannot avail or win him to it,
Then let him raise his gall up to his tongue,
And be as bitter as physicians' drugs, 55
Stretch his mouth wider with big swoll'n phrases.
Oh, here's a lad of mettle, stout Don Andrea,
Mettle to the crown,
Would shake the king's high court three handfuls down.

KING.
And well pick'd out, Knight Marshal; speech well strung; 60
I'd rather choose Horatio were he not so young.

HORATIO.
I humbly thank your highness,
In placing me next unto his royal bosom.

KING.
How stand ye, lords, to this election?

---

37. *repine*] feel discontent.
49. *politic*] crafty.
64. *election*] choice.

−5−

i   THE FIRST PART OF HIERONIMO

OMNES.
  Right pleasing, our dread sovereign.   65
MEDINA.
  Only with pardon, mighty sovereign,
  I should have chose Don Lorenzo.
CASTILE.
  I, Don Rogero.
ROGERO. Oh no; not me, my lords;
  I am war's champion, and my fees are swords;
  Pray, king, pray, peers, let it be Don Andrea; 70
  He's a worthy limb
  Loves wars and soldiers; therefore I love him.
HIERONIMO.
  And I love him, and thee, valiant Rogero;
  Noble spirits, gallant bloods,
  You are no wise insinuating lords,   75
  You ha' no tricks, you ha' none of all their sleights.
LORENZO [*aside*].
  So, so, Andrea must be sent ambassador?
  Lorenzo is not thought upon: good,
  I'll wake the court, or startle out some blood.
KING.
  How stand you, lords, to this election?   80
OMNES.
  Right pleasing, our dread sovereign.
KING.
  Then, Don Andrea—
ANDREA. My approved liege—
KING.
  We make thee our Lord High Ambassador.
ANDREA.
  Your highness circles me with honor's bounds.
  I will discharge the weight of your command 85
  With best respect; if friendly tempered phrase

67. I] *B; Castu.* I *Q, other edd.*   75. You are] *B;* your *Q.*
68. S.P. CASTILE. I] *B;* I *Q; Med.* 85. will] *B;* still *Q;* shall *Hz.*
I *other edd.*

71. *limb*] young man.

The First Part of Hieronimo

Cannot effect the virtue of your charge,
I will be heard like thunder, and as rough
As northern tempests, or the vexed bowels
Of too insulting waves, who at one blow   90
Five merchants' wealths into the deep doth throw.
I'll threaten crimson wars.

ROGERO.   Ay, ay, that's good;
Let them keep coin, pay tribute with their blood.

KING.
Farewell then, Don Andrea; to thy charge;
Lords, let us in; joy shall be now our guest;   95
Let's in to celebrate our second feast.   *Exeunt.*

Manet Lorenzo *solus.*

LORENZO.
Andrea's gone ambassador;
Lorenzo is not dreamt on in this age;
Hard fate,
When villains sit not in the highest state.   100
Ambition's plumes, that flourish'd in our court,
Severe Authority has dash'd with justice;
And Policy and Pride walk like two exiles,
Giving attendance, that were once attended,
And we rejected that were once high honored.   105
I hate Andrea, 'cause he aims at honor,
When my purest thoughts work in a pitchy vale,
Which are as different as heaven and hell.
One peers for day, the other gapes for night,
That yawning beldam with her jetty skin;   110
'Tis she I hug as mine effeminate bride,
For such complexions best appease my pride.

---

87. effect] *B;* affect *Q.*
88. heard] *this edn., conj. Brereton;* hard *Q, edd.*
89. vexed] *B;* vext *Q.*

95. let us] *B;* letes *Q.*
97–99.] *Q;* Lorenzo is...age;/ Andrea's gone ambassador; hard fate *conj. this edn.*

---

87. *virtue*] power, force.
90. *insulting*] exulting contemptuously.
104. *attended*] waited on; served.
112. *complexions*] (*a*) colors; (*b*) natures.

−7−

i   THE FIRST PART OF HIERONIMO

    I have a lad in pickle of this stamp,
    A melancholy, discontented courtier,
    Whose famish'd jaws look like the chap of death;   115
    Upon whose eyebrows hangs damnation;
    Whose hands are wash'd in rape, and murders bold.
    Him with a golden bait will I allure
    (For courtiers will do anything for gold)
    To be Andrea's death at his return: 120
    He loves my sister; that shall cost his life;
    So she a husband, he shall lose a wife.
    Oh sweet, sweet policy, I hug thee; good:
    Andrea's Hymen's draught shall be in blood.   *Exit.*

[ii]   *Enter* Horatio *at one door,* Andrea *at another.*

HORATIO.
    Whither in such haste, my second self?
ANDREA.
    I'faith, my dear bosom, to take solemn leave
    Of a most weeping creature.
HORATIO.   That's a woman.

            Enter Bel-imperia.

ANDREA.
    That's Bel-imperia.
HORATIO.   See, see, she meets you here:
    And what it is to love, and be loved dear!   5
BEL-IMPERIA.
    I have heard of your honor, gentle breast;
    I do not like it now so well, methinks.
ANDREA.
    What, not to have honor bestowed on me?
BEL-IMPERIA.
    Oh yes: but not a wand'ring honor, dear;

116. hangs] *Hz;* hang *Q.*   [ii]
                              5. it is] *edd.; except R, C, Hz* is it *Q.*

---

   113. *in pickle*] kept ready.
   115. *chap*] jaw.
[ii]
   7. *methinks*] it seems to me.

-8-

The First Part of Hieronimo

    I could afford it well, didst thou stay here.   10
    Could honor melt itself into thy veins,
    And thou the fountain, I could wish it so,
    If thou wouldst remain here with me, and not go.
ANDREA.
    'Tis but to Portugale.
HORATIO.
    But to demand the tribute, lady.
BEL-IMPERIA.   Tribute?   15
    Alas, that Spain cannot of peace forbear
    A little coin, the Indies being so near.
    And yet this is not all: I know you are too hot,
    Too full of spleen for an ambassador,
    And will lean much to honor.   20
ANDREA.
    Push!
BEL-IMPERIA.
    Nay, hear me, dear:
    I know you will be rough and violent,
    And Portingale hath a tempestuous son,
    Stamp'd with the mark of fury, and you two—   25
ANDREA.
    Sweet Bel-imperia!
BEL-IMPERIA.   Ye'll meet like thunder,
    Each imperious over other's spleen;
    You have both proud spirits and will strive to aspire;
    When two vex'd clouds jostle they strike out fire;
    And you, I fear me, war, which peace forfend.   30
    Oh dear Andrea, pray, let's have no wars.
    First let them pay the soldiers that were maim'd
    In the last battle, ere more wretches fall,
    Or walk on stilts to timeless funeral.
ANDREA.
    Respective dear, oh my life's happiness,   35

---

10. it well] *edd.;* well *Q.*   26. Ye'll] *this edn.;* Weele *Q;* You'll *R;* Youle *B.*
25. two—] *this edn., conj. Brereton;* too. *Q, edd.*   28. and] *this edn.;* and both *Q, edd.*

---

21. *Push!*] an exclamation of impatience.
24. *Portingale*] Portugal—a standard sixteenth-century form.
35. *Respective*] careful, anxious.

ii   THE FIRST PART OF HIERONIMO

    The joy of all my being, do not shape
    Frightful conceit beyond the intent of act.
    I know thy love is vigilant o'er my blood,
    And fears ill fate which heaven hath yet withstood.
    But be of comfort, sweet; Horatio knows   40
    I go to knit friends, not to kindle foes.
HORATIO.
    True, Madam Bel-imperia, that's his task:
    The phrase he useth must be gently styl'd,
    The king hath warned him to be smooth and mild.
BEL-IMPERIA.
    But will you indeed, Andrea?   45
ANDREA.
    By this, and by this lip-blushing kiss.
HORATIO.
    Oh, you swear sweetly.
BEL-IMPERIA.
    I'll keep your oath for you, till you return.
    Then I'll be sure you shall not be forsworn.

                Enter Pedringano.

ANDREA.
    Ho, Pedringano!   50
PEDRINGANO.
    Signioro.
ANDREA.
    Are all things aboard?
PEDRINGANO.
    They are, my good lord.
ANDREA.
    Then, Bel-imperia, I take leave: Horatio,
    Be in my absence my dear self, chaste self.   55
    What, playing the woman, Bel-imperia?
    Nay, then you love me not; or, at the least,
    You drown my honors in those flowing waters.

---

46. S.P. ANDREA. By ... kiss] *B;*   By this ... kisse *Q; And.* By this/
And. By this [*Bel.* catchword] *And.*   *Bel.* And this ... kiss *other edd.*

---

37. *conceit*] imagination.
52. *aboard*] Kyd's knowledge of geography is uncertain. Cf. iv.90.

−10−

The First Part of Hieronimo   iii

    Believe it, Bel-imperia, 'tis as common
    To weep at parting as to be a woman.   60
    Love me more valiant; play not this moist prize;
    Be woman in all parts, save in thy eyes.
    And so I leave thee.
BEL-IMPERIA.   Farewell, my lord:
    Be mindful of my love, and of your word.
ANDREA.
    'Tis fixed upon my heart; adieu, soul's friend.   65
HORATIO.
    All honor on Andrea's steps attend.
BEL-IMPERIA.
    Yet he is in sight, and yet—but now he's vanish'd.
                                          Exit Andrea.
HORATIO.
    Nay, lady, if you stoop so much to passion,
    I'll call him back again.
BEL-IMPERIA.   Oh, good Horatio, no:
    It is for honor; prithee let him go.   70
HORATIO.
    Then, madam, be compos'd, as you were wont,
    To music and delight: the time being comic will
    Seem short and pleasant till his return
    From Portingale: and, madam, in this circle
    Let your heart move;   75
    Honor'd promotion is the sap of love.   *Exeunt omnes.*

[iii]   *Enter* Lorenzo *and* Lazarotto, *a discontented courtier.*

LORENZO.
    Come, my soul's spaniel, my life's jetty substance,
    What's thy name?
LAZAROTTO.
    My name's an honest name, a courtier's name:
    'Tis Lazarotto.
LORENZO.   What, Lazarotto?

---

    61. *play not . . . prize*] do not contend publicly for a prize: here, make such a public show of weeping.
    72. *comic*] full of happiness and mirth.

—11—

iii   THE FIRST PART OF HIERONIMO

LAZAROTTO.
    Or rather rotting in this lazy age,   5
    That yields me no employments; I have mischief
    Within my breast, more than my bulk can hold:
    I want a midwife to deliver it.
LORENZO.
    I'll be the he one then, and rid thee soon
    Of this dull, leaden, and tormenting elf.   10
    Thou know'st the love
    Betwixt Bel-imperia and Andrea's bosom?
LAZAROTTO.
    Ay, I do.
LORENZO.
    How might I cross it, my sweet mischief?
    Honey damnation, how?
LAZAROTTO.   Well: 15
    As many ways as there are paths to hell,
    And that's enow, i'faith: from usurers' doors
    There goes one path: from friars' that nurse whores
    There goes another path: from brokers' stalls,
    From rich that die and build no hospitals,   20
    Two other paths: from farmers' that crack barns
    With stuffing corn, yet starve the needy swarms,
    Another path: from drinking schools one: one
    From dicing houses: but from the court, none, none.
LORENZO.
    Here is a slave just o'the stamp I wish,   25
    Whose inky soul is blacker than his name,
    Though it stand printed with a raven's quill.
    But, Lazarotto, cross my sister's love,
    And I'll rain showers of ducats in thy palm.
LAZAROTTO.
    Oh ducats, dainty ducks: for, give me ducats,   30

17. doors] *edd.;* doore *Q*.   27. printed] *Q;* painted *B*.
23. one: one] *B;* one *Q*.   30. for, give] *B;* forgive *Q, other*
26. inky soul is] *this edn., conj.* *edd.*
Brereton; Incke-soules *Q*.

---

  6. *mischief*] wickedness.   7. *bulk*] belly, trunk.
 10. *elf*] child.   17. *enow*] enough.

–12–

THE FIRST PART OF HIERONIMO   iii

    I'll fetch you duck enough; for gold and chink
    Makes the punk wanton and the bawd to wink.
LORENZO.
    Discharge, discharge, good Lazarotto, how
    We may cross my sister's loving hopes.
LAZAROTTO.   Nay, now,
    I'll tell you—   35
LORENZO.
    Thou knowest Andrea's gone ambassador.
LAZAROTTO.
    The better there is opportunity:
    Now list to me.
        Enter Hieronimo *and* Horatio, *and overhears their talk.*
    Alcario, the Duke Medina's son,
    Dotes on your sister, Bel-imperia;   40
    Him in her private gallery you shall place,
    To court her; let his protestations be
    Fashioned with rich jewels, for in love
    Great gifts and gold have the best tongue to move.
    Let him not spare an oath without a jewel   45
    To bind it fast: oh, I know women's hearts
    What stuff they are made of, my lord: gifts and giving
    Will melt the chastest-seeming female living.
LORENZO.
    Indeed Andrea is but poor, though honorable;
    His bounty amongst soldiers soaks him dry,   50
    And therefore great gifts may bewitch her eye.
HIERONIMO.
    Here's no fine villainy, no damn'd brother.
LORENZO.
    But, say she should deny his gifts, be all
    Compos'd of hate, as my mind gives me that she will:
    What then?   55

37. there is] *B;* thers *Q.*

---

  32. *wink*] close her eyes (to what happens).
  33. *Discharge*] reveal, express.
  54. *gives me*] forebodes.

−13−

iii   THE FIRST PART OF HIERONIMO

LAZAROTTO.
   Then thus: at his return to Spain,
   I'll murder Don Andrea.
LORENZO.   Dar'st thou, spirit?
LAZAROTTO.
   What dares not he do that ne'er hopes to inherit?
HORATIO.
   He dares be damn'd like thee.
LAZAROTTO.   Dare I? Ha! ha!
   I have no hope of everlasting height;   60
   My soul's a Moor, you know, salvation's white.
   What dare not I enact, then? Tush, he dies.
   I will make way to Bel-imperia's eyes.
LORENZO.
   To weep, I fear, but not to tender love.
LAZAROTTO.
   Why, is she not a woman? she must weep   65
   Awhile, as widows use, till their first sleep;
   Who in the morrow following will be sold
   To new, before the first are throughly cold.
   So Bel-imperia; for this is common;
   The more she weeps, the more she plays the woman.   70
LORENZO.
   Come then, howe'er it hap, Andrea shall be cross'd.
LAZAROTTO.
   Let me alone; I'll turn him to a ghost.

         Exeunt Lorenzo *and* Lazarotto. *Manent* Hieronimo *and* Horatio.

HIERONIMO.
   Farewell, true brace of villains;
   Come hither, boy Horatio, didst thou hear them?
HORATIO.
   Oh my true-breasted father,   75
   My ears have suck'd in poison, deadly poison.
   Murder Andrea! Oh inhuman practice!

72.1. Lazarotto ... Horatio.] *edd.;*   Lazarotto *and* Horatio. *Manet*
                                        Ieronimo. *Q.*

77. *practice*] plotting.

-14-

Had not your reverend years been present here,
I should have poniarded the villain's bowels,
And shoved his soul out to damnation. 80
Murder Andrea, honest lord! Impious villains!
HIERONIMO.
I like thy true heart, boy; thou lovest thy friend:
It is the greatest argument and sign
That I begot thee, for it shows thou art mine.
HORATIO.
Oh father, 'tis a charitable deed 85
To prevent those that would make virtue bleed.
I'll dispatch letters to Don Andrea;
Unfold their hellish practice, damn'd intent
Against the virtuous rivers of his life.
Murder Andrea!

Enter Isabella.

HIERONIMO. Peace: who comes here? News, 90
News, Isabella.
ISABELLA. What news, Hieronimo?
HIERONIMO.
Strange news: Lorenzo is become an honest man.
ISABELLA.
Is this your wondrous news?
HIERONIMO. Ay, is't not wondrous
To have honesty in hell? Go, tell it abroad now;
But see you put no new additions to it, 95
As thus—"Shall I tell you, gossip? Lorenzo is
Become an honest man:"—Beware, beware;
For honesty,
Spoken in derision, points out knavery.
Oh, then, take heed; that jest would not be trim; 100
He's a great man, therefore we must not knave him.
In, gentle soul; I'll not be long away,
As short my body, short shall be my stay. *Exit* Isabella.

93. Ay, is't] *B;* I if *Q;* Is it *R, C,*
Hz.

---

96. *gossip*] crony.
103. *short my body*] Cf. l. 114; vi.65; x.33, 37, 46; xiii.10–11.

−15−

THE FIRST PART OF HIERONIMO

HORATIO.
    Murder, Andrea! What blood-sucking slave
    Could choke bright honor in a scabbard grave? 105
HIERONIMO.
    What, harping still upon Andrea's death?
    Have courage, boy: I shall prevent their plots,
    And make them both stand like two politic sots.
HORATIO.
    Lorenzo has a reach as far as hell,
    To hook the devil from his flaming cell. 110
    Oh, sprightly father, he'll outreach you then;
    Knaves longer reaches have than honest men.
HIERONIMO.
    But, boy, fear not, I will outstretch them all;
    My mind's a giant, though my bulk be small.   *Exeunt omnes.*

[iv]

Enter the King of Portingale, Balthazar, Alexandro, Don Villuppo, *and others: a peal of ordnance within; a great shout of people.*

KING.
    What is the meaning of this loud report?
ALEXANDRO.
    An ambassador, my lord, is new arrived from Spain.
KING.
    Son Balthazar, we pray, do you go meet him,
    And do him all the honor that belongs him.
BALTHAZAR.
    Father, my best endeavor shall obey you.— 5
    Welcome, worthy lord, Spain's choice ambassador,
    Brave, stout Andrea, for so I guess thee.

Enter Andrea.

108. two] *this edn.;* too *Q.*   [iv]
113. I will] *B;* Ile *Q.*   2. ambassador] *B;* embas. *Q;*
114. small] *R;* full *Q.*   embassy *R, C, Hz.*

---

105. *scabbard*] scabbed, loathsome.
107. *prevent*] anticipate.

−16−

ANDREA.
>   Portugal's heir, I thank thee;
>   Thou seems no less than what thou art, a prince,
>   And an heroic spirit; Portingale's king,
>   I kiss thy hand, and tender on thy throne
>   My master's love, peace, and affection.

KING.
>   And we receive them, and thee, worthy Andrea;
>   Thy master's high-prized love unto our heart
>   Is welcome to his friend, thou to our court.

ANDREA.
>   Thanks, Portingale. My lords, I had in charge,
>   At my depart from Spain, this embassage,
>   To put your breast in mind of tribute due
>   Unto our master's kingdom these three years
>   Detained and kept back: and I am sent to know
>   Whether neglect, or will, detains it so.

KING.
>   Thus much return unto thy king, Andrea:
>   We have with best advice thought of our state,
>   And find it much dishonor'd by base homage.
>   I not deny but tribute hath been due to Spain
>   By our forefathers' base captivity:
>   Yet cannot rase't out their successors' merit?
>   'Tis said we shall not answer at next birth
>   Our fathers' faults in heaven; why then on earth?
>   Which proves and shows, that which they lost by base
>   captivity,
>   We may redeem with honored valiancy.
>   We borrow nought; our kingdom is our own:
>   He is a base king that pays rent for his throne.

ANDREA.
>   Is this thy answer, Portingale?

BALTHAZAR.
>   Ay, Spain;
>   A royal answer too, which I'll maintain.

11. thy hand] *B;* my hand *Q.*   27. rase't] *B;* raze *Q.*
20. I am] *R;* I *Q.*   27. merit?] *B;* merit: *Q.*

27. *rase't out*] eliminate it.

iv   The First Part of Hieronimo

OMNES.
    And all the peers of Portugale the like.
ANDREA.
    Then thus all Spain, which but three minutes ago
    Was thy full friend, is now returned thy foe.
BALTHAZAR.
    An excellent foe; we shall have scuffling good.
ANDREA.
    Thou shalt pay tribute, Portugale, with blood.   40
BALTHAZAR.
    Tribute for tribute, then: and foes for foes.
ANDREA.
    I bid you sudden wars.
BALTHAZAR.   I, sudden blows,
    And that's as good as wars. Don, I'll not bate
    An inch of courage nor a hair of fate.
    Pay tribute? Ay, with strokes.
ANDREA.   Ay, with strokes you shall.   45
    Alas, that Spain should correct Portugal!
BALTHAZAR.
    Correct?
    In that one word such torments do I feel
    That I could lash thy ribs with valiant steel.
ANDREA.
    Prince Balthazar, shall's meet?   50
BALTHAZAR.
    Meet, Don Andrea? Yes, in the battle's bowels:
    Here is my gage, a never-failing pawn;
    'Twill keep his day, his hour, nay minute; 'twill.
ANDREA.
    Then thine and this possess one quality.
BALTHAZAR.
    Oh, let them kiss,   55
    Did I not understand thee noble, valiant,
    And worthy my sword's society with thee,

---

45. S.P. ANDREA. Ay, with...   48. In] *this edn.;* O in *Q, edd.*
shall] *Q, edd.;* ANDREA. With...   52. Here is] *B;* Heres *Q.*
shall *conj. this edn.*

---

38. *returned*] again turned.

  For all Spain's wealth I'd not grasp hands.
  Meet, Don Andrea? I tell thee, noble spirit,
  I'd wade up to the knees in blood,   60
  I'd make a bridge of Spanish carcasses,
  To single thee out of the gasping army.
ANDREA.
  Woo't thou, prince? why even for that I love thee.
BALTHAZAR.
  Tut, love me, man, when we have drunk
  Hot blood together; wounds will tie   65
  An everlasting settled amity,
  And so shall thine.
ANDREA.   And thine.
BALTHAZAR.   What, give no place?
ANDREA.
  To whom?
BALTHAZAR.   To me.
ANDREA.   To thee? Why should my face
  That's placed above my mind, fall under it?
BALTHAZAR.
  I'll make thee yield.
ANDREA.   Ay, when you get me down;   70
  But I stand even yet, jump crown to crown.
BALTHAZAR.
  Dar'st thou?
ANDREA.   I dare.
BALTHAZAR.   I am all vex'd.
ANDREA.   I care not.
BALTHAZAR.
  I shall forget the law.
ANDREA.   Do, do.
BALTHAZAR.   Shall I?
ANDREA.   Spare not.
BALTHAZAR.
  But thou wilt yield first.

63. love thee] *B;* loue *Q.*

---

63. *Woo't*] wilt.
71. *jump*] exactly.
72. *vex'd*] agitated.

iv   The First Part of Hieronimo

ANDREA.   No.
BALTHAZAR.   I hug thee for't,
    The valiant'st spirit e'er trod the Spanish court.   75
ALEXANDRO.
    My liege, two nobler spirits never met.
BALTHAZAR.
    Here let the rising of our hot blood set,
    Until we meet in purple, when our swords
    Shall——
ANDREA.
    Agreed, right valiant prince.   80
    Then, Portugale, this is thy resolute answer?
KING.
    So return; it's so: we have bethought us
    What tribute is; how poor that monarch shows
    Who for his throne a yearly pension owes:
    And what our predecessors lost to Spain   85
    We have fresh spirits that can renew it again.
ANDREA.
    Then I unclasp the purple leaves of war:
    Many a new wound must gasp through an old scar.
    So, Portugale, I leave thee.
KING.   Our self in person
    Will see thee safe aboard. Come, son, come lords,   90
    Instead of tribute we must pay our swords.
BALTHAZAR.
    Remember, Don Andrea, that we meet—
ANDREA.
    Up hither sailing in a crimson fleet.   *Exeunt omnes.*

[v]   *Enter* Lorenzo *and* Alcario.

LORENZO.
    Do you affect my sister?
ALCARIO.
    Affect? above affection, for her breast

---

74. I] *this edn.;* O, I Q, *edd.*   76, 77] *edd.; lines transposed in Q.*

[v]
  1. *affect*] love.

Is my life's treasure; oh entire
Is the condition of my hot desire.

LORENZO.
Then this must be your plot. 5
You know Andrea's gone ambassador,
On whom my sister Bel-imperia
Casts her affection.
You are in stature like him, speech alike;
And had you but his vestment on your back, 10
There's no one living but would swear 'twere he:
Therefore, sly policy must be your guide.
I have a suit just of Andrea's colors,
Proportion'd in all parts—nay, twins his own:
This suit within my closet shall you wear, 15
And so disguis'd, woo, sue, and then at last—

ALCARIO.
What?

LORENZO.
Obtain thy love.

ALCARIO.
This falls out rare; in this disguise I may
Both wed, bed, and board her? 20

LORENZO.
You may, you may.
Besides, within these few days he'll return.

ALCARIO.
Till this be acted I in passion burn.

LORENZO.
All falls out for the purpose: all hits jump;
The date of his embassage nigh expired 25
Gives strength unto our plot.

ALCARIO.
True, true; all to the purpose.

LORENZO.
Moreover, I will buzz Andrea's landing,
Which, once but crept into the vulgar mouths,

14. twins] *B*; twas *Q*.   18. thy] *R;* my *Q*.

3. *entire*] total, unlimited.   15. *closet*] private room.
28. *buzz*] rumor abroad.   29. *vulgar*] of the common people.

V   The First Part of Hieronimo

      Is hurried here and there, and sworn for troth;   30
      Think, 'tis your love makes me create this guise,
      And willing hope to see your virtue rise.
ALCARIO.
      Lorenzo's bounty I do more infold
      Than the greatest mine of India's brightest gold.
LORENZO.
      Come, let us in; the next time you shall show   35
      All Don Andrea, not Alcario.   *Exeunt omnes.*

[vi]

      Enter Hieronimo *trussing of his points,* Horatio *with pen and ink.*

HIERONIMO.
      Come, pull the table this way; so, 'tis well:
      Come, write, Horatio, write:
      This speedy letter must away tonight.

          Horatio *folds the paper the contrary way.*

      What, fold paper that way to a noble man?
      To Don Andrea, Spain's ambassador?   5
      Fie! I am ashamed to see it.
      Hast thou worn gowns in the university,
      Toss'd logic, suck'd philosophy,
      Eat cues, drunk cees, and cannot give a letter
      The right courtier's crest? Oh there's a kind of state   10
      In everything, save in a cuckold's pate.
      Fie, fie, Horatio: what, is your pen foul?
HORATIO.
      No, father, cleaner than Lorenzo's soul;
      That's dipp'd in ink made of an envious gall;
      Else had my pen no cause to write at all.   15

34. India's] *R, C, Hz;* Indians *Q,*   [vi]
other edd.   8. Toss'd] *edd.;* Lost *Q.*

    0.1. *trussing . . . points*] tying the points or laces fastening the lower to the upper garments.
    8. *Toss'd logic*] "bandied words in logical disputations" (B).
    9. *cues . . . cees*] University terms for small quantities of bread and beer; a *cue* (q=quadrans) is a farthing's worth.
    14. *gall*] (*a*) bile, bitterness; (*b*) an ingredient of ink.

−22−

HIERONIMO.
    "Signior Andrea," say.
HORATIO.
    "Signior Andrea."
HIERONIMO.
    "'Tis a villainous age this."
HORATIO.
    "'Tis a villainous age this."
HIERONIMO.
    "That a nobleman should be a knave as well as an ostler."   20
HORATIO.
    "That a nobleman should be a knave as well as an ostler."
HIERONIMO.
    "Or a serjeant."
HORATIO.
    "Or a serjeant."
HIERONIMO.
    "Or a broker."
HORATIO.
    "Or a broker."   25
HIEROMINO.
    "Yet I speak not this of Lorenzo, for he's an honest lord."
HORATIO.
    "'Sfoot, father, I'll not write him 'honest lord.'"
HIERONIMO.
    Take up thy pen, or I'll take up thee.
HORATIO.
    What, write him "honest lord"? I'll not agree.
HIERONIMO.
    You'll take it up, sir.   30
HORATIO.
    Well, well.
HIERONIMO.
    What went before? Thou hast put me out:
    Beshrew thy impudence or insolence.
HORATIO.
    "Lorenzo's an honest lord."

---

22. *serjeant*] law officer.
28. *I'll take up*] I'll rebuke, reprove.

HIERONIMO.
Well, sir;—"and has hired one to murder you." 35
HORATIO.
Oh, I cry you mercy, father, meant you so?
HIERONIMO.
Art thou a scholar, Don Horatio,
And canst not aim at figurative speech?
HORATIO.
I pray you, pardon me; 'twas but youth's hasty error.
HIERONIMO.
Come, read then. 40
HORATIO.
"And has hired one to murder you."
HIERONIMO.
"He means to send you to heaven, when you return from Portugale."
HORATIO.
"From Portugale."
HIERONIMO.
"Yet he's an honest duke's son." 45
HORATIO.
"Yet he's an"—
HIERONIMO.
"But not the honest son of a duke."
HORATIO.
"But not the honest"—
HIERONIMO.
"Oh, that villainy should be found in the great chamber."
HORATIO.
"Oh, that villainy"— 50
HIERONIMO.
"And honesty in the bottom of a cellar."
HORATIO.
"And honesty"—
HIERONIMO.
"If you'll be murdered, you may."
HORATIO.
"If you'll be"—

---

49. *great chamber*] reception or audience room in a palace.

HIERONIMO.
"If you be not, thank God and Hieronimo."   55
HORATIO.
"If you be not"—
HIERONIMO.
"If you be, thank the devil and Lorenzo."
HORATIO.
"If you be, thank"—
HIERONIMO.
"Thus hoping you will not be murder'd, and you can choose."
HORATIO.
"Thus hoping you will"—   60
HIERONIMO.
"Especially being warned beforehand."
HORATIO.
"Especially"—
HIERONIMO.
"I take my leave,"—boy Horatio, write "leave" bending in the hams like an old courtier— "Thy assured friend," say, "'gainst Lorenzo and the devil, little Hieronimo, Marshal."   65
HORATIO.
"Hieronimo, Marshal."
HIERONIMO.
So, now read it o'er.
HORATIO.
"Signior Andrea, 'tis a villainous age this, that a nobleman should be a knave as well as an ostler, or a serjeant, or a broker; yet I speak not this of Lorenzo; he's an honest lord,   70
and has hired one to murder you, when you return from Portugale: yet he's an honest duke's son, but not the honest son of a duke. Oh, that villainy should be found in the great chamber, and honesty in the bottom of a cellar."
HIERONIMO.
True, boy: there's a moral in that; as much to say, knavery   75
in the court and honesty in a cheese-house.
HORATIO.
"If you'll be murdered, you may: if you be not, thank God

63. leave,"—boy] *B*; leave boy *Q*,   63-65, 68-74.] *as doggerel in Q.* other edd.

—25—

and Hieronimo: if you be, thank the devil and Lorenzo. Thus hoping you will not be murdered, and you can choose, especially being warned beforehand, I take my leave." 80

HIERONIMO.
  Horatio, hast thou written "leave" bending in the hams enough, like a gentleman usher? 'Sfoot, no, Horatio; thou hast made him straddle too much like a Frenchman: for shame, put his legs closer, though it be painful. 85

HORATIO.
  So: 'tis done, 'tis done—"Thy assured friend 'gainst Lorenzo and the devil, little Hieronimo, Marshal."

Enter Lorenzo *and* Isabella.

ISABELLA.
  Yonder he is, my lord; pray you speak to him.

HIERONIMO.
  Wax, wax, Horatio: I had need wax too;
  Our foes will stride else over me and you. 90

ISABELLA.
  He's writing a love-letter to some Spanish lady,
  And now he calls for wax to seal it.

LORENZO.
  God save you, good Knight Marshal.

HIERONIMO.
  Who's this? my lord Lorenzo? welcome, welcome;
  You're the last man I thought on, save the devil: 95
  Much doth your presence grace our homely roof.

LORENZO.
  Oh Hieronimo,
  Your wife condemns you of a uncourtesy,
  And over-passing wrong; and more, she names
  Love-letters which you send to Spanish dames. 100

HIERONIMO.
  Do you accuse me so, kind Isabella?

ISABELLA.
  Unkind Hieronimo.

---

99. *over-passing*] surpassing, excessive.

LORENZO.
>And, for my instance, this in your hand is one.

HIERONIMO.
>In sooth, my lord, there is no written name
>Of any lady, then no Spanish dame. 105

LORENZO.
>If it were not so, you would not be afeard
>To read or show the wax'd letter:
>Pray you, let me behold it.

HIERONIMO.
>I pray you, pardon me:
>I must confess, my lord, it treats of love, 110
>Love to Andrea, ay, even to his very bosom.

LORENZO.
>What news, my lord, hear you from Portugale?

HIERONIMO.
>Who, I? before your grace it must not be;
>The badger feeds not till the lion's served:
>Nor fits it news so soon kiss subject's ears 115
>As the fair cheek of high authority.
>Hieronimo lives much absent from the court,
>And being absent there, lives from report.

LORENZO.
>Farewell, Hieronimo.

ISABELLA.
>Well, come, my lord Lorenzo. 120

> *Exeunt* Lorenzo *and* Isabella.

HIERONIMO.
>Boy,
>Thy mother's jealous of my love to her.

HORATIO.
>Oh she play'd us a wise part; now ten to one
>He had not overheard the letter read,
>Just as he enter'd.

115. subject's ears] *R;* subjects *Q.*   *Brereton;* Welcome, *Q, edd.*
120. Well, come] *this edn., conj.*   120.1.] *this edn.; after l. 119 in Q.*

---

103. *instance*] example, proof.
122. *jealous*] suspicious.

−27−

HIERONIMO.   Though it had happen'd evil, 125
    He should have heard his name yok'd with the devil.
    Here, seal the letter with a loving knot;
    Send it with speed, Horatio, linger not,
    That Don Andrea may prevent his death,
    And know his enemy by his envious breath.   *Exeunt omnes.* 130

[vii]   *Enter* Lorenzo, *and* Alcario *disguis'd like* Andrea.

LORENZO.
    Now, by the honor of Castile's true house,
    You are as like Andrea, part for part,
    As he is like himself: did I not know you,
    By my cross I swear, I could not think you but
    Andrea's self, so legg'd, so fac'd, so speech'd, 5
    So all in all: methinks I should salute
    Your quick return and speedy haste from Portugale:
    Welcome, fair lord, worthy ambassador,
    Brave Don Andrea. —Oh, I laugh to see
    How we shall jest at her mistaking thee. 10

ALCARIO.
    What, have you given it out Andrea is return'd?

LORENZO.
    'Tis all about the court in every ear,
    And my invention brought to me for news
    Last night at supper: and which the more to cover,
    I took a bowl and quaff'd a health to him, 15
    When it would scarce go down for extreme laughter
    To think how soon report had scatter'd it.

ALCARIO.
    But is the villain Lazarotto
    Acquainted with our drift?

LORENZO.   Not for Spain's wealth;
    Though he be secret, yet suspect the worst, 20
    For confidence confounds the stratagem.
    The fewer in a plot of jealousy

3. I not] *R;* I *Q*.   20. suspect] *B;* suspects *Q*.

---

    4. *cross*] formed by the hilt of his sword.
   13. *my invention*] the false rumor I spread.
   21. *confounds*] destroys, frustrates.

The First Part of Hieronimo

    Build a foundation surest, when multitudes
    Makes it confused ere it come to head.
    Be secret, then; trust not the open air,   25
    For air is breath, and breath-blown words raise care.

ALCARIO.
    This is the gallery where she most frequents;
    Within this walk have I beheld her dally
    With my shape's substance. Oh, immortal powers,
    Lend your assistance; clap a silver tongue   30
    Within this palate, that, when I approach
    Within the presence of this demi-goddess,
    I may possess an adamantic power,
    And so bewitch her with my honey'd speech;
    Have every syllable a music stop,   35
    That, when I pause, the melody may move
    And hem persuasion 'tween her snowy paps,
    That her heart hearing may relent and yield.

LORENZO.
    Break off, my lord: see, where she makes approach.

Enter Bel-imperia.

ALCARIO.
    Then fall into your former vein of terms.   40

LORENZO.
    Welcome, my lord;
    Welcome, brave Don Andrea, Spain's best of spirit.
    What news from Portugale? tribute or war?
    But see, my sister Bel-imperia comes:
    I will defer it till some other time,   45
    For company hinders love's conference.   *Exit* Lorenzo.

BEL-IMPERIA.
    Welcome, my life's self form, dear Don Andrea.

ALCARIO.
    My words iterated gives thee as much:
    Welcome, my self of self.

---

27. S.P. ALCARIO. This] *B;* This *Q.*   *other edd.*
28. Within] *Q, B; Alc.* Within *R,*   40. vein] *edd.;* vaines *Q.*

    29. *my shape's substance*] the real Andrea.
    33. *adamantic*] magnetic; the diamond (adamant) or loadstone was then supposed to have this power.

vii   THE FIRST PART OF HIERONIMO

BEL-IMPERIA.
    What news, Andrea? Treats it peace or war?   50
ALCARIO.
    At first they cried all war, as men resolved
    To lose both life and honor at one cast:
    At which I thunder'd words all clad in proof
    Which struck amazement to their palled speech,
    And tribute presently was yielded up.   55
    But, Madam Bel-imperia, leave we this,
    And talk of former suits and quests of love.

            They whisper. Enter Lazarotto.

LAZAROTTO.
    'Tis all about the court Andrea's come:
    Would I might greet him; and I wonder much
    My lord Lorenzo is so slack in murder   60
    Not to afford me notice all this while.
    Gold, I am true;
    I had my hire, and thou shall have thy due.
    Was't possible to miss him so? Soft, soft,
    This gallery leads to Bell-imperia's lodging;   65
    There he is, sure, or will be, sure; I'll stay:
    The evening too begins to slubber day;
    Sweet, opportuneful season; here I'll lean
    Like a court hound that licks fat trenchers clean.
BEL-IMPERIA.
    But has the king partook your embassy?   70
ALCARIO.
    That till tomorrow shall be now deferr'd.
BEL-IMPERIA.
    Nay, then you love me not:
    Let that be first dispatch'd;
    Till when receive this token.
                      She kisses him. Exit Bel-imperia.

74.1.] *edd.; after l. 73 in Q.*

---

    53. *proof*] armor.
    54. *palled*] appalled.
    67. *slubber*] obscure.
    70. *partook*] shared the news of.

THE FIRST PART OF HIERONIMO   vii

ALCARIO.
    I to the king with this unfaithful heart?   75
    It must not be; I play too false a part.
LAZAROTTO.
    Up, Lazarotto; yonder comes thy prize:
    Now lives Andrea, now Andrea dies.
                Lazarotto *kills him.*
ALCARIO.
    That villain Lazarotto has kill'd me
    Instead of Andrea.   80
           Enter Andrea, *and* Rogero, *and others.*
ROGERO.
    Welcome home, Lord Ambassador.
ALCARIO.
    Oh, oh, oh!
ANDREA.
    Whose groan was that? What frightful villain's this,
    His sword unsheathed? Whom hast thou murder'd, slave?
LAZAROTTO.
    Why—Don—Don Andrea.   85
ANDREA.
    No, counterfeiting villain.
    He says, my lord, that he hath murdered me.
LAZAROTTO.
    Ay, Don Andrea, or else Don the devil.
ANDREA.
    Lay hands on him; and some
    Rear up the bleeding body to the light.   90
ROGERO.
    My lord, I think 'tis you; were you not here,
    A man might swear 'twere you.
ANDREA.
    His garments, ha! like mine; his face made like.
    An ominous horror all my veins doth strike.
    Sure, this pretends my death; this misery   95
    Aims at some fatal pointed tragedy.

80.1. *others*] *edd.;* other *Q.*   89. and some] *B;* some *Q.*

---

95. *pretends*] portends.
96. *pointed*] appointed.

vii   THE FIRST PART OF HIERONIMO

Enter Hieronimo *and* Horatio.

HIERONIMO.
    Son Horatio, see Andrea slain!
HORATIO.
    Andrea slain? Then, weapon, cling my breast.
ANDREA.
    Live, truest friend, forever loved and blest.
HORATIO.
    Lives Don Andrea?
ANDREA.   Ay; but slain in thought   100
    To see so strange a likeness forged and wrought.
    Lords, cannot you yet descry
    Who is the owner of this red, melting body?
ROGERO.
    My lord,
    It is Alcario, Duke Medina's son;   105
    I know him by this mole upon his breast.
LAZAROTTO.
    Alcario slain? Hast thou beguil'd me, sword?
    Arm, hast thou slain thy bountiful, kind lord?
    Why then rot off, and drop upon the ground,
    Strew all the galleries with gobbets round.   110

            Enter Lorenzo.

LORENZO.
    Who names Alcario slain? It is Alcario.
    Oh cursed deed:
    Couldst thou not see, but make the wrong man bleed?
LAZAROTTO.
    'Sfoot, 'twas your fault, my lord; you brought no word.
LORENZO.
    Peace; no words; I'll get thy pardon.   115
    Why, mum then.

            Enter Bel-imperia.

BEL-IMPERIA.
    Who names Andrea slain? Oh, 'tis Andrea:
    Oh, I sound, I die.

---

  98. *cling*] cleave, pierce.
  118. *sound*] swoon.

−32−

LORENZO.
>Look to my sister, Bel-imperia.

ANDREA.
>Raise up my dear love, Bel-imperia.　　　　　　120
>Oh, be of comfort, sweet, call in thy spirits;
>Andrea lives: oh, let not death beguile thee.

BEL-IMPERIA.
>Are you Andrea?

ANDREA.　　　　　　Do not forget
>That was Alcario, my shape's counterfeit.

LORENZO.
>Why speaks not this accursed, damned villain?　125

LAZAROTTO.
>Oh, good words, my lords, for those are courtier's veils.
>The king must hear; why should I make two tales,
>For to be found in two? Before the king
>I will resolve you all this strange, strange thing:
>I hot, yet miss'd; 'twas I mistook my part.　　　130

HORATIO.
>Ay, villain, for thou aim'd'st at this true heart.

HIERONIMO.
>Horatio, 'twas well, as fortune stands,
>This letter came not to Andrea's hands.

HORATIO.
>'Twas happiness indeed.

BEL-IMPERIA.
>Was it not you, Andrea, questioned me?　　　　135
>'Bout love?

ANDREA.　　　No, Bel-imperia;
>Belike 'twas false Andrea, for the first
>Object mine eyes met was that most accurst;
>Which, I much fear me, by all signs pretends
>Most doubtful wars and dangerous pointed ends　140
>To light upon my blood.

BEL-IMPERIA.
>Angels of heaven forfend it.

139. pretends] *edd.;* pretend *Q.*

---

128. *found*] found out.
130. *hot*] hit.

ANDREA.
>Some take up the body; others take charge
>Of that accursed villain.

LORENZO.
>My lord, leave that to me; I'll look to him. 145

HIERONIMO.
>Mark, mark, Horatio: a villain guard a villain.

ANDREA.
>The king may think my news is a bad guest,
>When the first object is a bleeding breast. *Exeunt omnes.*

[viii]
Enter King of Spain, *Castile*, Medina, *Rogero, and others* [Andrea, Lorenzo, Lazarotto, Hieronimo, Horatio, Lord General]; *a dead march within.*

KING.
>My lords,
>What heavy sounds are these, nearer, and nearer?
>Ha! Andrea, the forerunner of these news?
>Nay, then I fear Spain's inevitable ill.
>Ha! Andrea, speak; what news from Portugale? 5
>What, is tribute paid? is't peace or wars?

ANDREA.
>Wars, my dread liege.

KING.
>   Why then, that bleeding object
>Doth presage what shall hereafter follow;
>What's he that lies there slain, or hurt, or both?
>Speak. 10

ANDREA.
>My liege, Alcario, Duke Medina's son;
>And by that slave this purple act was done.

MEDINA.
>Who names Alcario slain? Ay me, 'tis he:
>Art thou that villain?

LAZAROTTO.
>   How didst know my name?
>I see an excellent villain hath his fame 15
>As well as a great courtier.

6. is't peace] *B;* peace *Q.*

---

2. *heavy*] sad, serious.

MEDINA.
    Speak, villain: wherefore didst thou this accursed deed?
LAZAROTTO.
    Because I was an ass, a villainous ass;
    For had I hot it right,
    Andrea had lain there, he walk'd upright;   20
    This ominous mistake, this damned error,
    Breeds in my soul an everlasting terror.
KING.
    Say, slave, how came this accursed evil?
LAZAROTTO.
    Faith, by myself, my short sword, and the devil.
    To tell you all without a tedious tongue,   25
    I'll cut them down, my words shall not be hung.
    That hapless, bleeding Lord Alcario,
    Which this hand slew, pox on't, was a huge doter
    On Bel-imperia's beauty, who replied
    In scorn, and his hot suit denied;   30
    For her affections were all firmly planted
    In Don Andrea's bosom; yet unwise
    He still pursued it with blind lover's eyes.
    Then hired he me with gold—oh fate, thou elf—
    To kill Andrea, which hire kill'd himself;   35
    For not content to stay the time of murder,
    He took Andrea's shape unknown to me,
    And in all parts disguised, as there you see,
    Intending, as it seemed, by that sly shift,
    To steal away her troth: short tale to tell,   40
    I took him for Andrea, down he fell.
KING.
    Oh impious deed,
    To make the heir of honor melt and bleed.
    Bear him away to execution.
LAZAROTTO [*aside to* Lorenzo].
    Nay, Lord Lorenzo, where's the pardon?   45
    'Sfoot, I'll peach else.

26. be hung] *B;* hang *Q;* hang long   35. hire] *Q;* here *R, C, Hz.*
R, C, Hz.

---

  20. *he*] Alcario.
  26. *cut . . . down*] (*a*) shorten; (*b*) remove from the gallows.
  46. *peach*] inform (slang).

LORENZO [*aside to* Lazarotto].
  Peace, Lazarotto, I'll get it of the king.
LAZAROTTO [*aside to* Lorenzo].
  Do't quickly then, or I'll spread villainy.
LORENZO [*aside to the* King].
  My lord, he is the most notorious rogue
  That ever breath'd.   *In his ear.*   50
KING.
  Away with him!
LORENZO.
  Your highness may do well to bar his speech;
  'Tis able to infect a virtuous ear.
KING.
  Away with him, I will not hear him speak.
LAZAROTTO.
  My lord Lorenzo is a ———   55

          They stop his mouth and bear him in.

HIERONIMO.
  Is not this a monstrous courtier?
HORATIO.
  He is the court toad, father.
KING.
  Tribute denied us, ha?
ANDREA.
  It is, my liege, and that with no mean words:
  He will redeem his honor lost with swords.   60
KING.
  So daring, ha! so peremptory?
  Can you remember the words he spake?
ANDREA.
  Word for word, my gracious sovereign,
  And these they were: "Thus much return to Spain:
  Say that our settled judgment hath advis'd us   65
  What tribute is, how poor that monarch shows
  Who for his throne a yearly pension owes;
  And what our predecessors lost to Spain
  We have fresh spirits that can renew it again."

55.1. *They*] i.e., Lorenzo and attendants.

−36−

KING.
> Ha, so peremptory, daring, stout? 70

ANDREA.
> Then, my liege,
> According to your gracious, dread command,
> I bade defiance with a vengeful hand.

KING.
> He entertained it?

ANDREA.
> Ay, and returned it with menacing brows: 75
> Prince Balthazar, his son,
> Grew violent, and wished the fight begun.

Enter Lorenzo.

LORENZO [*aside*].
> So, so, I have sent my slave to hell:
> Though he blab there, the devils will not tell.
> > *A tucket within.*

KING.
> How now, what means this trumpet's sound? 80

Enter a Messenger.

MESSENGER.
> My liege, the Portugales
> Are up in arms, glitt'ring in steel.

KING.
> Where's our lord general, Lorenzo, stout Andrea,
> With whom I rank sprightly Horatio?
> What, for shame, shall the Portugales 85
> Trample the fields before you?

GENERAL.
> > No, my liege,
> There's time enough to let out blood enough,
> Tribute shall flow
> Out of their bowels, and be tendered so.

KING.
> Farewell, brave lords; my wishes are bequeath'd; 90
> A nobler rank of spirits never breath'd.
> > *Exeunt* King *and Nobles.*

---

72. to your] *R;* your *Q.* 81–82. S.P. MESSENGER. My.../
80.1.] *edd.; after l. 81 in Q.* Are...] *edd.;* My.../ *Mess.* Are...
  Q.

79.1. *tucket*] a flourish of trumpets.

THE FIRST PART OF HIERONIMO

HIERONIMO.
    Oh, my sweet boy, heaven shield thee still from care;
    Oh, be as fortunate as thou art fair.
HORATIO.
    And heaven bless you, my father, in this fight,
    That I may see your gray head crown'd in white.   95
                                            Exeunt omnes.

[ix]   *Enter* Andrea *and* Bel-imperia.

BEL-IMPERIA.
    You came but now, and must you part again?
    You told me that your spirit should put on peace;
    But see, war follows war.
ANDREA.   Nay, sweet love, cease,
    To be denied our honor, why, 'twere base
    To breathe and live; and wars in such a case   5
    Is even as necessary as our blood.
    Swords are in season then when rights withstood.
    Deny us tribute that so many years
    We have in peace told out? why, it would raise
    Spleen in the host of angels: 'twere enough   10
    To make the tranquil saints of angry stuff.
BEL-IMPERIA.
    You have o'erwrought the chiding of my breast;
    And by that argument you firmly prove
    Honor to soar above the pitch of love.
    Lend me thy loving and thy warlike arm,   15
    On which I knit this soft and silken charm
    Tied with an amorous knot: oh, may it prove
    Enchanted armor being charmed by love;
    That when it mounts up to thy warlike crest,
    It may put by the sword, and so be blest.   20
ANDREA.
    Oh, what divinity proceeds from love!
    What happier fortune, then, myself can move?

93. thou] *edd.;* thee *Q.*   11. make the] *B;* make *Q;* make
[ix]   our *R, C, Hz.*
1. and must] *Hz;* must *Q.*

9. told] counted.

−38−

THE FIRST PART OF HIERONIMO

    Hark, the drum beckons me; sweet dear, farewell.
    This scarf shall be my charm 'gainst foes and hell.
BEL-IMPERIA.
    Oh, let me kiss thee first.
ANDREA.   The drum again!   25
BEL-IMPERIA.
    Hath that more power than I?
ANDREA.   Do't quickly then:
    Farewell.   *Exit* Andrea.
BEL-IMPERIA.   Farewell. Oh cruel part;
    Andrea's bosom bears away my heart.   *Exit* Bel-imperia.

[x]

Enter Balthazar, Alexandro, Villuppo, Don Pedro, *with soldiers, drum and colors.*

BALTHAZAR.
    Come, valiant spirits, you peers of Portugale,
    That owe your lives, your faiths, and services,
    To set you free from base captivity:
    Oh, let our fathers' scandal ne'er be seen
    As a base blush upon our free-born cheeks;   5
    Let all the tribute that proud Spain receiv'd
    Of all those captive Portugales deceased
    Turn into chafe, and choke their insolence.
    Methinks no moiety, not one little thought
    Of them whose servile acts live in their graves   10
    But should raise spleens big as a cannon bullet
    Within your bosoms: oh, for honor,
    Your country's reputation, your lives' freedom,
    Indeed your all that may be termed revenge,
    Now let your bloods be liberal as the sea;   15
    And all those wounds that you receive of Spain,
    Let theirs be equal to quit yours again.

---

5. our] *Q;* your *B.*   7. all those] *edd.;* those all *Q.*

---

  27. *part*] parting.
[x]
  8. *chafe*] rage, passion.   17. *quit*] requite, repay.

x   THE FIRST PART OF HIERONIMO

    Speak, Portugales: are you resolved as I,
    To live like captives, or as free-born die?
VILLUPPO.
    Prince Balthazar, as you say, so say we—   20
    To die with honor, scorn captivity.
BALTHAZAR.
    Why, spoke like true Portugales indeed;
    I am assured of your forwardness.
    Now, Spain, sit firm; I'll make thy towers shake,
    And all that gold thou hadst from Portugale,   25
    Which makes thy court melt in luxuriousness,
    I vow to have it treble at thy hands.
    Hark, Portugales: I hear their Spanish drum.
    March on, and meet them; this must be the day
    That all they have received they back must pay.   30
                            The Portugales march about.

Enter Hieronimo, Andrea, Horatio, Lorenzo, Lord General, Rogero, *and attendants with drum and colors.*

HIERONIMO.
    What, are you braving us before we come?
    We'll be as shrill as you: strike alarm, drum.
                      They sound a flourish o' both sides.
BALTHAZAR.
    Thou inch of Spain;
    Thou man, from thy hose downward, scarce so much;
    Thou very little longer than thy beard;   35
    Speak not such big words;
    They'll throw thee down, little Hieronimo;
    Words greater than thyself, it must not be.
HIERONIMO.
    And, thou long thing of Portugale, why not?
    Thou, that art full as tall   40
    As an English gallows, upper beam and all;
    Devourer of apparel, thou huge swallower,
    My hose will scarce make thee a standing collar.
    What, have I almost quited you?
ANDREA.
    Have done, impatient Marshal.

38. not be] *Hz;* not *Q;* be *R, C.*

BALTHAZAR.   Spanish combatants,   45
    What, do you set a little pygmire marshal
    To question with a prince?
ANDREA.   No, Prince Balthazar,
    I have desired him peace, that we might war.
    What, is the tribute money tender'd yet?
BALTHAZAR.
    Tribute, ha! ha! What else? Wherefore meet our drums   50
    But for to tender and receive the sums
    Of many a bleeding heart, which ere sunfall,
    Shall pay dear tribute, even their lives and all.
ANDREA.
    Prince Balthazar, I know your valiant spirit,
    I know your courage to be tried and good;   55
    Yet, oh prince, be not confirmed in blood.
    Not that I taste of fear or cowardice,
    But of religion, piety, and love
    To many bosoms that yet firmly move
    Without disturbed spleens. Oh, in thy heart,   60
    Weigh the dear drops of many a purple part
    That must be acted on the field's green stage,
    Before the evening dews quench the sun's rage.
    Let tribute be appeased and so stayed,
    And let not wonted fealty be denayed   65
    To our desertful kingdom. Portugales,
    Keep your forefathers' oaths; that virtue craves;
    Let them not lie forsworn now in their graves,
    To make their ashes perjur'd and unjust,
    For heaven can be revenged on their dust.   70
    They swore to Spain, both for themselves and you,
    And will posterity prove their sires untrue?
    This should not be 'mong men of virtuous spirit.
    Pay tribute thou, and receive peace and merit.
BALTHAZAR.
    Oh virtuous coward!

---

51. But for] *B;* But *Q.*   74. merit] *this edn.;* writ *Q, edd.*
65. denayed] *R;* denied *Q.*

---

46. *pygmire*] pigmy.
65. *denayed*] denied.

—41—

HORATIO.   Oh ignoble spirit,   75
    To term him coward for his virtuous merit!
ANDREA.
    Coward? Nay then, relentless rib of steel,
    What virtue cannot, thou shalt make him feel.
LORENZO.
    Proud Alexandro, thou art mine.
ALEXANDRO.   Agreed.
ROGERO.
    And thou, Villuppo, mine.
VILLUPPO.   I'll make thee bleed.   80
HORATIO.
    And thou, Don Pedro, mine.
PEDRO.   I care not whose,
    Or thine, or thine, or all at once.
BALTHAZAR.
    I bind thee, Don Andrea, by thy honor,
    Thy valiancy, and all that thou hold'st great,
    To meet me single in the battle's heat,   85
    Where I'll set down, in characters on thy flesh,
    Four precious lines, spoke by our father's mouth,
    When first thou cam'st ambassador; these they are:
    " 'Tis said we shall not answer at next birth
    Our fathers' faults in heaven, why then on earth?   90
    Which proves and shows that what they lost by base
        captivity,
    We may redeem with wonted valiancy."
    And to this crimson end our colors spread;
    Our courages are new born, our valors bred.
    Therefore, Andrea, as thou tender'st fame,   95
    War's reputation, and a soldier's name,
    Meet me.
ANDREA.   I will.
BALTHAZAR.   Single me out.
ANDREA.   I shall.

---

86. on] *edd.;* vpon *Q.*   96. War's reputation] *this edn.;*
94. courages] *edd.;* courage *Q.*   Wars, reputation *Q, edd.*

---

86. *characters*] letters.

ALEXANDRO.
　　Do you the like.
LORENZO.　　　　　And you all, and we.
ANDREA.
　　Can we be foes, and all so well agreed?
BALTHAZAR.
　　Why, man, in war there's bleeding amity;　　　　100
　　And he this day gives me the deepest wound,
　　I'll call him brother.
ANDREA.　　　　　　Then, prince, call me so;
　　To gain that name, I'll give the deepest blow.
HIERONIMO.
　　Nay, then, if brotherhood by strokes come due,
　　I hope, boy, thou wilt gain a brother too.　　　　105
HORATIO.
　　Father, I doubt it not.
ANDREA.　　　　　Lord General,
　　Breathe like your name, a general defiance
　　'Gainst Portugale.
GENERAL.　　　Defiance to the Portugales!
BALTHAZAR.
　　The like breathe our Lord General 'gainst the Spaniards.
GENERAL.
　　Defiance to the Spaniards!
ANDREA.　　　　　　Now cease words;　　　　110
　　I long to hear the music of clashed swords.
BALTHAZAR.
　　Why, thou shalt hear it presently.

　　　　　　　They offer to fight.

ANDREA.　　　　　　　Quickly then.
BALTHAZAR.
　　Why now.
GENERAL.　　Oh stay, my lords,
　　This will but breed a mutiny in the camp.
BALTHAZAR.
　　I am all fire, Andrea.

102. Then] *R;* The *Q.*

ANDREA. Art thou? good: 115
Why, then, I'll quench thee, prince, with thine own blood.
BALTHAZAR.
Adieu.
ANDREA. Adieu.
BALTHAZAR. Let's meet. *Exit* Balthazar.
ANDREA. 'Tis meet we did. *Exeunt* Portugales.
LORENZO.
Alexandro!
ALEXANDRO.
Lorenzo!
ROGERO.
Villuppo! 120
VILLUPPO.
Rogero!
HORATIO.
Don Pedro!
PEDRO.
Horatio!
HIERONIMO.
Ay, ay, Don Pedro, my boy shall meet thee.
Come, valiant spirits of Spain, 125
Valiant Andrea, fortunate Lorenzo,
Worthy Rogero, sprightly Horatio—
Oh let me dwell a little on that name—
Be all as fortunate as heaven's blest host,
But blame me not, I'd have Horatio most. 130
Ride home all conquerors, when the fight is done,
Especially ride thee home so, my son.
So now kiss and embrace: come, come,
I am war's tutor; strike alarum, drum. *Exeunt omnes.*

[xi]

After a long alarm, the Portugales *and* Spaniards *meet. The* Portugales *are put to the worst.*

Enter Hieronimo *solus.*

HIERONIMO.
Oh valiant boy; struck with a giant's arm
His sword so falls upon the Portugales,

117. S.D. *Exit* Balthazar.] *after l. 116*   131. Ride home] *B;* Ride *Q.* in *Q.*

-44-

THE FIRST PART OF HIERONIMO   xi

    As he would slice them out like oranges,
    And squeeze their bloods out. Oh abundant joy,
    Never had father a more happier boy.   *Exit* Hieronimo.   5

          Enter Balthazar *and a Soldier.*

BALTHAZAR.
    Can you not find me Don Andrea forth?
    Oh for a voice shriller than all the trumpets,
    To pierce Andrea's ears through the hot army.
    Go, search again; bring him, or ne'er return.   *Exit* Soldier.
    Valiant Andrea, by thy worthy blood,   10
    Thy honored faith, which thou pawn'd'st to mine,
    By all that thou hold'st dear upon this earth,
    Sweat now to find me in the height of blood.
    Now death doth heap his goods up all at once,
    And crams his store house to the top with blood;   15
    Might I now and Andrea in one fight
    Make up thy wardrobe richer by a knight—
    Who's that? Andrea?

          Enter Rogero.

ROGERO.
    Ha, Villuppo!
BALTHAZAR.
    No; but a better.   20
ROGERO.
    Pox on't!
BALTHAZAR.
    Pize on't!
    What luck is this: but sir, you part not so;
    Whate'er you be, I'll have a bout with you.
ROGERO.
    Content: this is joy mixed with spite,   25
    To miss a lord, and meet a prince in fight.
BALTHAZAR.
    Come, meet me, sir.

3. As] *Hz;* As if *Q.*   18. Who's that? Andrea?] *Q; not*
6. find me] *B;* finde *Q.*   *in R, C, Hz; Bal.* Whose that?
8. pierce] *R;* prince *Q.*   Andrea? *B.*

22. *Pize*] a mild oath.

—45—

ROGERO.
    Just halfway; I'll meet it with my sword.

        They fight. Balthazar *beats in* Rogero.

          Enter Andrea *with a* Captain.

ANDREA.
    Where might I find this valorous Balthazar,
    This fierce courageous prince, a noble worthy,   30
    Made of the ribs of Mars and fortitude?
    He promised to meet fair, and single me
    Out o' the misty battle. Did you search
    The left wing for him? Speak!

CAPTAIN.   We did, my lord.

ANDREA.
    And could he not be found?

CAPTAIN.   Not in that wing, my lord.   35

ANDREA.
    Why, this would vex
    The resolution of a suffering spleen.
    Prince Balthazar, Portugal's valiant heir,
    The glory of our foe, the heart of courage,
    The very soul of true nobility.   40
    I call thee by thy right name, answer me.
    Go, captain, pass the left wing squadron; hie.
    Mingle yourself again amidst the army;
    Pray sweat to find him out.   *Exit* Captain.
              This place I'll keep:
    Now wounds are wide, and blood is very deep: 45
    'Tis now about the heavy dread of battle;
    Soldiers drop down as thick as if death mowed them;
    As scythemen trim the long-hair'd ruffian fields,
    So fast they fall, so fast to fate life yields.

              Enter Balthazar.

BALTHAZAR.
    I have sweat much, yet cannot find him. —Andrea!   50

ANDREA.
    Prince Balthazar:
    Oh, lucky minute!

BALTHAZAR.   Oh long wished-for hour!
    Are you remember'd, Don, of a daring message,

And a proud attempt?
You braved me, Don, within my father's court. 55
ANDREA.
   I think I did.
BALTHAZAR.   This sword shall lash you for it.
ANDREA.
   Alas!
   War knows I am too proud a scholar grown,
   Now to be lashed with steel; had I not known
   My strength and courage, it had been easy then 60
   To have me borne upon the backs of men.
   But now—I am sorry, prince—you come too late;
   That were proud steel, i'faith, that should do that.
BALTHAZAR.
   I can hold no longer:
   Come, come, let's see which of our strengths is stronger. 65
ANDREA.
   Mine for a wager.
BALTHAZAR.   Thine? What wager, say?
ANDREA.
   I hold three wounds to one.
BALTHAZAR.   Content: a lay;
   But you shall keep stakes then.
ANDREA.   Nay, I'll trust you,
   For you're a prince; I know you'll pay your due.
BALTHAZAR.
   I'll pay it you soundly.
ANDREA.   Prince, you might have paid 70
   Tribute as well; then battles had been stayed.
BALTHAZAR.
   Here's tribute for you.
ANDREA.   I'll receive it of you,
   And give you acquittance with a wound or two.

   They fight. Balthazar *hath* Andrea *down.*
Enter Hieronimo *and* Horatio. Horatio *beats away* Balthazar.

ANDREA.
   Thou art a wondrous friend, a happy spirit;

---

67. *lay*] wager.

xi THE FIRST PART OF HIERONIMO

    I owe thee now my life. Couldst thou inherit   75
Within my bosom, all I have is thine;
For by this act I hold thy arm divine.
HORATIO.
    Are you not wounded? let me search and see.
ANDREA.
    No, my dear self, for I was bless'd by thee.
Else his unpitying sword had cleft my heart,   80
Had not Horatio play'd some angel's part.
Come, happy mortal, let me rank by thee,
Then am I sure no star will threaten me.
HORATIO.
    Let's to the battle once more; we may meet
This haughty prince, and wound him at our feet.   85
                        Exeunt omnes.

    Enter Rogero *and* Alexandro *in their shirts, with poleaxes.*

ROGERO.
    Art thou true valiant? Hast thou no coat of proof
Girt to thy loins? Art thou true loyal?
ALEXANDRO.   Why look:
    Witness the naked truth upon my breast.
Come let's meet, let's meet,
And break our haughty skulls down to our feet.   90

        They fight. Alexandro *beats in* Rogero.

Enter Lorenzo *and* Don Pedro *at one door, and* Alexandro *and* Rogero *at another door.* Lorenzo *kills* Don Pedro, *and* Alexandro *kills* Rogero. *Enter at one door* Andrea, *at another door* Balthazar.

ANDREA.
    Oh me ill stead, valiant Rogero slain!
BALTHAZAR.
    Oh my sad fates, Don Pedro welt'ring in his gore!
Oh could I meet Andrea, now my blood's
A-tiptoe, this hand and sword should melt him:
Valiant Don Pedro!   95

83. am I] *Q;* I am *B.*

---

86. *proof*] mail.

ANDREA.
>Worthy Rogero, sure 'twas multitudes
>That made thee stoop to death; one Portugale
>Could ne'er o'erwhelm thee in such crimson streams:
>And no mean blood shall quit it. Balthazar,
>Prince Balthazar!

BALTHAZAR. Andrea, we meet in blood now. 100

ANDREA.
>Ay, in valiant blood of Don Rogero's shedding,
>And each drop worth a thousand Portugales.

BALTHAZAR.
>I'll top thy head for that ambitious word.

ANDREA.
>You cannot, prince: see, a revengeful sword
>Waves o'er my head.

BALTHAZAR. Another over mine: 105
>Let them both meet in crimson tincture's shine.

They fight and Andrea *hath* Balthazar *down. Enter* Portugales *and relieve* Balthazar *and kill* Andrea.

ANDREA.
>Oh, I am slain; help me, Horatio!
>My foes are base, and slay me cowardly;
>Farewell dear, dearest Bel-imperia!
>Yet herein joy is mingled with sad death: 110
>I keep her favor longer than my breath. *He dies.*

Sound alarm. Andrea *slain, and* Prince Balthazar *vaunting on him. Enter* Hieronimo, Horatio, *and Lord General.*

HORATIO.
>My other soul, my bosom, my heart's friend,
>Oh my Andrea slain! I'll have the price
>Of him in princely blood, Prince Balthazar.
>My sword shall strike true strains, 115
>And fetch Andrea's ransom forth thy veins.
>Lord General, drive them hence while I make war.
>>[*Exit Lord General.*]

102. worth] *B;* is worth *Q.*   117. S.D.] *this edn.; not in Q.*
113. Oh my] *Q* (My O).

103. *top*] cut off.

BALTHAZAR.
>Hath war made thee so impudent and young?
>My sword shall give correction to thy tongue.

HIERONIMO.
>Correct thy rascals, prince; thou correct him? 120
>Lug with him, boy; honors in blood best swim.

They fight and breathe afresh.

BALTHAZAR.
>So young and valorous; this arm ne'er met
>So strong a courage of so green a set.

HORATIO.
>If thou be'st valiant, cease these idle words,
>And let revenge hang on our glittering swords, 125
>With this proud prince, the haughty Balthazar.

Horatio *has* Prince Balthazar *down; then enter* Lorenzo *and seizes his weapons.*

>Hand off, Lorenzo, touch not my prisoner.

LORENZO.
>He's my prisoner; I seiz'd his weapons first.

HORATIO.
>Oh base renown,
>'Tis easy to seize those were first laid down. 130

LORENZO.
>My lance first threw him from his warlike steed.

HIERONIMO.
>Thy lance, Lorenzo? Now, by my beard, you lie.

HORATIO.
>Well, my lord,
>To you awhile I tender my whole prisoner.

LORENZO.
>Horatio, 135
>You tender me part of mine own, you know.

HORATIO.
>Well, peace; with my blood dispense,
>Until my liege shall end the difference.

130. were first] *B;* were forst *Q, R;* whom force *conj. Hz.*

HIERONIMO.
>Lorenzo, thou dost boast of base renown;
>Why, I could whip all these, were their hose down.   140

HORATIO.
>Speak, prince, to whether dost thou yield?

BALTHAZAR.
>The vanquish'd yields to both, to you the first.

HORATIO.
>Oh abject prince! what, dost thou yield to two?

HIERONIMO.
>Content thee, boy; thou shalt sustain no wrong.
>I'll to the king before, and let him know   145
>The sum of victory, and his overthrow.   *Exit* Hieronimo.

LORENZO.
>Andrea slain, thanks to the stars above!
>I'll choose my sister out her second love.
>   *Exeunt* Lorenzo *and* Balthazar.

HORATIO.
>Come, noble rib of honor, valiant carcass,
>I loved thee so entirely, when thou breathed'st,   150
>That I could die, were't but to bleed with thee,
>And wish me wounds, even for society.
>Heaven and this arm once saved thee from thy foe,
>When his all-wrathful sword did basely point
>At the rich circle of thy laboring heart,   155
>Thou grovelling under indignation
>Of sword and ruth. Oh then stepp'd heaven and I
>Between the stroke, but now alack must die:
>Since so the powers above have writ it down
>In marble leaves that death is mortal crown.   160
>Come then, my friend, in purple I will bear
>Thee to my private tent, and then prepare
>For honor'd funeral for thy melting corse.

He takes his scarf and ties it about his arm.

142. the first] *Hz;* first *Q.*   160. crown] *edd.;* crownd *Q.*

---

141. *whether*] which of the two; cf. Mathew 21:31: "whether of them twain..."
152. *society*] companionship.
160. *death...crown*] Finis coronat opus: cf. *Spanish Tragedy,* II.vi.8.

−51−

xi   THE FIRST PART OF HIERONIMO

    This scarf I'll wear in memory of our souls,
    And of our mutual loves; here, here, I'll wind it,   165
    And full as often as I think on thee,
    I'll kiss this little ensign, this soft banner,
    Smear'd with foes' blood, all for the master's honor.
    Alas, I pity Bel-imperia's eyes;
    Just at this instant her heart sinks and dies.   170

Exit Horatio *carrying* Andrea *on his back. Enter* Hieronimo *solus.*

HIERONIMO.
    My boy adds treble comfort to my age;
    His share is greatest in this victory.
    The Portugales are slain and put to flight,
    By Spaniards' force, most by Horatio's might.
    I'll to the Spanish tents to see my son,   175
    Give him my blessing, and then all is done. [*Exit* Hieronimo.]

[xii]

Enter two, dragging of ensigns; then the funeral of Andrea: *next* Horatio *and* Lorenzo, *leading* Prince Balthazar *captive; then the Lord General with others mourning. A great cry within,* "Charon, a boat, a boat." *Then enter* Charon *and the ghost of* Andrea[, *and* Revenge].

HORATIO.
    Oh, my lords,
    See, Don Andrea's ghost salutes me, see, embraces me.
LORENZO.
    It is your love that shapes this apprehension.
HORATIO.
    Do you not see him plainly, lords?
    Now he would kiss my cheek. Oh my pale friend,   5
    Wert thou anything but a ghost, I could love thee.
    See, he points at his own hearse—mark, all—
    As if he did rejoice at funeral.
ANDREA.
    Revenge, give my tongue freedom to paint her part,
    To thank Horatio, and commend his heart.   10

176. S.D.]. *this edn.; not in Q*.   3. apprehension] *Q;* apparition *R,*
[xii]   *C.*
0.4. *and* Revenge] *B; not in Q.*

    0.3. *Charon*] who ferries the souls across the river Styx to Hades.

THE FIRST PART OF HIERONIMO

REVENGE.
    No, you'll blab secrets then.
ANDREA.
    By Charon's boat, I will not.
REVENGE.
    Nay, you shall not: therefore pass;
    Secrets in hell are lock'd with doors of brass:
    Use action, if you will, but not in voice;   15
    Your friend conceives in signs how you rejoice.
HORATIO.
    See, see, he points to have us go forward on.
    I prithee, rest; it shall be done, sweet Don.
    Oh, now he's vanish'd.

        Sound trumpets, and a peal of ordnance.

ANDREA.   I am a happy ghost;
    Revenge, my passage now cannot be cross'd.   20
    Come, Charon; come, hell's sculler, waft me o'er
    Yon sable streams, which look like molten pitch;
    My funeral rites are made, my hearse hung rich.
        Exeunt Ghost *and* Revenge. *A great noise within.*
WITHIN.
    Charon, a boat; Charon! Charon!
CHARON.
    Who calls so loud on Charon?   25
    Indeed 'tis such a time, the truth to tell,
    I never want a fare to pass to hell.   *Exeunt omnes.*

[xiii]
Sound a flourish. Enter marching Horatio *and* Lorenzo, *leading* Prince Balthazar; Lord General, *Phillippo, and Cassimero, with followers.*

HORATIO.
    These honor'd rites and worthy duties spent
    Upon the funeral of Andrea's dust,

17. us] *R*; his *Q*.   22. Yon] *B*; you *Q*; your *R*, *later edd.*

0.2. *Phillippo, Cassimero*] not elsewhere mentioned, and mute.

—53—

xiii   THE FIRST PART OF HIERONIMO

        Those once his valiant ashes—march we now
        Homeward with victory to crown Spain's brow.
GENERAL.
        The day is ours and joy yields happy treasure;   5
        Set on to Spain in most triumphant measure.   *Exeunt omnes.*

             Enter Hieronimo *solus.*

HIERONIMO.
        'Fore God, I have just miss'd them: ha!
        Soft, Hieronimo! thou hast more friends
        To take thy leave of. Look well about thee,
        Embrace them, and take friendly leave. My arms   10
        Are of the shortest; let your loves piece them out.
        You're welcome, all, as I am a gentleman;
        For my son's sake, grant me a man at least;
        At least I am. So good-night, kind gentles,
        For I hope there's never a Jew among you all;   15
        And so I leave you.   *Exit.*

THE SPANISH TRAGEDY

[DRAMATIS PERSONAE

GHOST OF ANDREA, *a Spanish Courtier* ⎫
REVENGE ⎭ in Induction and Chorus

KING OF SPAIN
DON CYPRIAN, *Duke of Castile, his brother*
LORENZO, *the Duke's son*
BEL-IMPERIA, *Lorenzo's sister*
PEDRINGANO, *Bel-imperia's servant*
LORENZO'S PAGE

VICEROY OF PORTUGAL
DON PEDRO, *his brother*
BALTHAZAR, *the Viceroy's son*
SERBERINE, *Balthazar's servant*

HIERONIMO, *Marshal of Spain*
ISABELLA, *his wife*
HORATIO, *their son*
ISABELLA'S MAID

SPANISH GENERAL
DEPUTY (*Judge*)
PORTUGUESE AMBASSADOR
ALEXANDRO ⎫
VILLUPPO ⎭ *Portuguese noblemen*

BAZULTO, *an old man*
CHRISTOPHIL, *Bel-imperia's janitor*
HANGMAN
MESSENGER
THREE WATCHMEN
TWO PORTUGUESE

SOLIMAN, *Sultan of Turkey* (by Balthazar) ⎫
ERASTUS, *Knight of Rhodes* (by Lorenzo) ⎬ in Hieronimo's Play
THE BASHAW (by Hieronimo) ⎪
PERSEDA (by Bel-imperia) ⎭

A DRUM
THREE KINGS ⎫
THREE KNIGHTS ⎭ in First Dumb Show

—57—

The Spanish Tragedy

HYMEN
TWO TORCH BEARERS } in Second Dumb Show

BAZARDO, *a Painter*
PEDRO } *Hieronimo's servants* } in the Additions to the play
JACQUES
THREE CITIZENS

ARMY, ROYAL SUITES, NOBLES, OFFICERS, HALBERDIERS, SERVANTS, TRUMPETS, &c.]

Dramatis Personae] *adapted from Boas.*

The Spanish Tragedy

[or

Hieronimo is Mad Again]

[I.i] [INDUCTION]

Enter the Ghost of Andrea, *and with him* Revenge.

ANDREA.
When this eternal substance of my soul
Did live imprison'd in my wanton flesh,
Each in their function serving other's need,
I was a courtier in the Spanish court.
My name was Don Andrea; my descent, 5
Though not ignoble, yet inferior far
To gracious fortunes of my tender youth.
For there in prime and pride of all my years,
By duteous service and deserving love,
In secret I possess'd a worthy dame, 10
Which hight sweet Bel-imperia by name.
But in the harvest of my summer joys
Death's winter nipp'd the blossoms of my bliss,
Forcing divorce betwixt my love and me.
For in the late conflict with Portingale 15
My valor drew me into danger's mouth
Till life to death made passage through my wounds.

---

2. *wanton*] unrestrained, sportive.
10. *In secret...dame*] See II.i.45–50; III.x.54–55; III.xiv.111–112; and Introduction, pp. xvii–xviii.
11. *hight*] was called.
15. *the late conflict*] See *1 Hieronimo, passim*.
15. *Portingale*] Portugal—a standard sixteenth-century form.

I.i   The Spanish Tragedy

When I was slain, my soul descended straight
To pass the flowing stream of Acheron;
But churlish Charon, only boatman there,   20
Said that, my rites of burial not perform'd,
I might not sit amongst his passengers.
Ere Sol had slept three nights in Thetis' lap,
And slak'd his smoking chariot in her flood,
By Don Horatio, our Knight Marshal's son,   25
My funerals and obsequies were done.
Then was the ferryman of Hell content
To pass me over to the slimy strond
That leads to fell Avernus' ugly waves.
There, pleasing Cerberus with honied speech,   30
I pass'd the perils of the foremost porch.
Not far from hence, amidst ten thousand souls,
Sat Minos, Aeacus, and Rhadamanth;
To whom no sooner 'gan I make approach,
To crave a passport for my wand'ring ghost,   35
But Minos, in graven leaves of lottery,
Drew forth the manner of my life and death.
"This knight," quoth he, "both liv'd and died in love,
And for his love tried fortune of the wars,
And by war's fortune lost both love and life."   40
"Why then," said Aeacus, "convey him hence,
To walk with lovers in our fields of love,
And spend the course of everlasting time
Under green myrtle trees and cypress shades."
"No, no," said Rhadamanth, "it were not well   45
With loving souls to place a martialist.
He died in war, and must to martial fields,
Where wounded Hector lives in lasting pain,
And Achilles' Myrmidons do scour the plain."
Then Minos, mildest censor of the three,   50

18–85.] Based on Virgil *Aeneid* vi.
20. *Charon*] See *1 Hieronimo*, scene xii.
25. *Knight Marshal*] a law officer of the king's household.
28. *strond*] strand.
33. *Minos, Aeacus, Rhadamanth*] judges of Hades.
36. *of lottery*] describing his lot on earth.
46. *martialist*] warrior; one who has lived by war.

Made this device to end the difference:
"Send him," quoth he, "to our infernal king,
To doom him as best seems his majesty."
To this effect my passport straight was drawn.
In keeping on my way to Pluto's court, 55
Through dreadful shades of ever-glooming night,
I saw more sights than thousand tongues can tell,
Or pens can write, or mortal hearts can think.
Three ways there were: that on the right-hand side
Was ready way unto the 'foresaid fields, 60
Where lovers live and bloody martialists,
But either sort contain'd within his bounds.
The left-hand path, declining fearfully,
Was ready downfall to the deepest hell,
Where bloody Furies shakes their whips of steel, 65
And poor Ixion turns an endless wheel;
Where usurers are chok'd with melting gold,
And wantons are embrac'd with ugly snakes,
And murderers groan with never-killing wounds,
And perjur'd wights scalded in boiling lead, 70
And all foul sins with torments overwhelm'd.
'Twixt these two ways I trod the middle path,
Which brought me to the fair Elysian green,
In midst whereof there stands a stately tower,
The walls of brass, the gates of adamant. 75
Here finding Pluto with his Proserpine,
I showed my passport, humbled on my knee;
Whereat fair Proserpine began to smile,
And begg'd that only she might give my doom.
Pluto was pleas'd, and seal'd it with a kiss. 80
Forthwith, Revenge, she rounded thee in th'ear,
And bade thee lead me through the gates of horn,
Where dreams have passage in the silent night.

---

53. *doom*] judge.
62. *his*] its.
64. *downfall*] descent.
75. *adamant*] diamond.
81. *rounded*] whispered.
82. *gates of horn*] from these, in Virgil *Aeneid* vi.893–896, true dreams issue; from the gates of ivory, false dreams—the twin gates of sleep.

I.i   THE SPANISH TRAGEDY

  No sooner had she spoke but we were here,
  I wot not how, in twinkling of an eye.   85
REVENGE.
  Then know, Andrea, that thou art arriv'd
  Where thou shalt see the author of thy death,
  Don Balthazar, the Prince of Portingale,
  Depriv'd of life by Bel-imperia.
  Here sit we down to see the mystery,   90
  And serve for Chorus in this tragedy.

[I.ii]   *Enter* Spanish King, General, Castile, Hieronimo.
KING.
  Now say, Lord General, how fares our camp?
GENERAL.
  All well, my sovereign liege, except some few
  That are deceas'd by fortune of the war.
KING.
  But what portends thy cheerful countenance,
  And posting to our presence thus in haste?   5
  Speak, man, hath fortune given us victory?
GENERAL.
  Victory, my liege, and that with little loss.
KING.
  Our Portingals will pay us tribute then?
GENERAL.
  Tribute and wonted homage therewithal.
KING.
  Then bless'd be heaven and guider of the heavens,   10
  From whose fair influence such justice flows.
CASTILE.
  O multum dilecte Deo, tibi militat aether,
  Et conjuratae curvato poplite gentes
  Succumbunt: recti soror est victoria juris.

---

13. *poplite*] *Q2, 4–10;* poplito *Q1, 3.*

 90. *mystery*] events with a secret meaning.
[I.ii]
 1. *camp*] army (or campaign).
 12–14.] "Oh much loved of God, for thee heaven fights, and the conspiring peoples fall on bended knee; victory is the sister of just right." Adapted from Claudian, *De Tertio Consulatu Honorii,* ll. 96–98.

KING.
>Thanks to my loving brother of Castile.— 15
>But, General, unfold in brief discourse
>Your form of battle and your war's success,
>That, adding all the pleasure of thy news
>Unto the height of former happiness,
>With deeper wage and greater dignity 20
>We may reward thy blissful chivalry.

GENERAL.
>Where Spain and Portingale do jointly knit
>Their frontiers, leaning on each other's bound,
>There met our armies in their proud array;
>Both furnish'd well, both full of hope and fear, 25
>Both menacing alike with daring shows,
>Both vaunting sundry colors of device,
>Both cheerly sounding trumpets, drums, and fifes,
>Both raising dreadful clamors to the sky,
>That valleys, hills, and rivers made rebound, 30
>And heaven itself was frighted with the sound.
>Our battles both were pitch'd in squadron form,
>Each corner strongly fenc'd with wings of shot;
>But ere we join'd and came to push of pike,
>I brought a squadron of our readiest shot 35
>From out our rearward to begin the fight.
>They brought another wing to encounter us.
>Meanwhile, our ordnance played on either side,
>And captains strove to have their valors tried.
>Don Pedro, their chief horsemen's colonel, 40
>Did with his cornet bravely make attempt

38. ordnance] *Q 9-10;* ordinance *Q 1-8.*

---

20. *wage*] wages, reward.
21. *chivalry*] prowess in war.
27. *colors of device*] heraldic banners.
30. *That*] so that.
32. *battles*] battalions.
32. *squadron*] square.
33. *shot*] troops with firearms.
34. *push of pike*] close fighting.
40. *colonel*] trisyllabic.
41. *cornet*] troop of cavalry (from the standard at its head).

I.ii   THE SPANISH TRAGEDY

  To break the order of our battle ranks;
  But Don Rogero, worthy man of war,
  March'd forth against him with our musketeers,
  And stopp'd the malice of his fell approach. 45
  While they maintain hot skirmish to and fro,
  Both battles join and fall to handy-blows,
  Their violent shot resembling th'ocean's rage,
  When, roaring loud, and with a swelling tide,
  It beats upon the rampires of huge rocks 50
  And gapes to swallow neighbor-bounding lands.
  Now, while Bellona rageth here and there,
  Thick storms of bullets rain like winter's hail,
  And shivered lances dark the troubled air.
    Pede pes et cuspide cuspis; 55
    Arma sonant armis, vir petiturque viro.
  On every side drop captains to the ground,
  And soldiers, some ill-maim'd, some slain outright;
  Here falls a body scindered from his head,
  There legs and arms lie bleeding on the grass, 60
  Mingled with weapons and unbowell'd steeds,
  That scattering overspread the purple plain.
  In all this turmoil, three long hours and more,
  The victory to neither part inclin'd;
  Till Don Andrea, with his brave lanciers, 65
  In their main battle made so great a breach,
  That, half dismay'd, the multitude retir'd;
  But Balthazar, the Portingales' young prince,
  Brought rescue and encourag'd them to stay.
  Here-hence the fight was eagerly renew'd, 70

53. rain] *C;* ran *Qq;* run *conj. M.* 59. scindered] *Q 1–3* (scindred); sundered *Q 4–10.*

---

 47. *handy-blows*] hand-to-hand fighting.
 50. *rampires*] ramparts.
 55–56.] "Foot against foot and lance against lance; arms clash on arms, and man is attacked by man."
 59. *scindered*] sundered.
 61. *unbowell'd*] disembowelled.
 65. *lanciers*] lancers.
 70. *Here-hence*] because of this (*OED*).

–64–

The Spanish Tragedy   I.ii

And in that conflict was Andrea slain,
Brave man at arms, but weak to Balthazar.
Yet while the Prince, insulting over him,
Breath'd out proud vaunts, sounding to our reproach,
Friendship and hardy valor, join'd in one, 75
Prick'd forth Horatio, our Knight Marshal's son,
To challenge forth that prince in single fight.
Not long between these twain the fight endur'd,
But straight the prince was beaten from his horse,
And forc'd to yield him prisoner to his foe. 80
When he was taken, all the rest they fled,
And our carbines pursued them to the death,
Till, Phoebus waning to the western deep,
Our trumpeters were charg'd to sound retreat.

KING.
Thanks, good Lord General, for these good news; 85
And for some argument of more to come,
Take this and wear it for thy sovereign's sake.
Give him his chain.
But tell me now, hast thou confirm'd a peace?

GENERAL.
No peace, my liege, but peace conditional,
That if with homage tribute be well paid, 90
The fury of your forces will be stay'd;
And to this peace their viceroy hath subscrib'd,
Give the King *a paper.*
And made a solemn vow that, during life,
His tribute shall be truly paid to Spain.

KING.
These words, these deeds, become thy person well. 95
But now, Knight Marshal, frolic with thy king,
For 'tis thy son that wins this battle's prize.

---

83. waning] *Q5–10, conj. MSR4;*   87.1. *Give*] *Q1;* Giues *Q2–10.*
wauing *Q1–4.*   92.1. *Give*] *Q1–3;* Giues *Q4–10.*

---

72. *to*] compared with.
73. *insulting*] exulting insolently.
76. *Prick'd*] spurred.
86. *argument*] earnest; pledge.
96. *frolic*] be merry; rejoice.

I.ii   THE SPANISH TRAGEDY

HIERONIMO.
  Long may he live to serve my sovereign liege,
  And soon decay, unless he serve my liege.   *A tucket afar off.*
KING.
  Nor thou nor he shall die without reward.—   100
  What means the warning of this trumpet's sound?
GENERAL.
  This tells me that your grace's men of war,
  Such as war's fortune hath reserv'd from death,
  Come marching on towards your royal seat,
  To show themselves before your majesty;   105
  For so I gave in charge at my depart.
  Whereby by demonstration shall appear
  That all, except three hundred or few more,
  Are safe return'd, and by their foes enrich'd.

      The Army enters; Balthazar, *between* Lorenzo *and* Horatio, *captive.*

KING.
  A gladsome sight! I long to see them here.   110
            They enter and pass by.
  Was that the warlike prince of Portingale,
  That by our nephew was in triumph led?
GENERAL.
  It was, my liege, the prince of Portingale.
KING.
  But what was he that on the other side
  Held him by th'arm, as partner of the prize?   115
HIERONIMO.
  That was my son, my gracious sovereign;
  Of whom though from his tender infancy
  My loving thoughts did never hope but well,
  He never pleas'd his father's eyes till now,
  Nor fill'd my heart with overcloying joys.   120
KING.
  Go, let them march once more about these walls,

---

99. S.D. *tucket*] *Q1–2; Trumpet*   101. this] *Q1–6;* the *Q7–10.*
Q3–10.   106. in] *Q1–3, 5;* them *Q4, 6–10.*
101. the] *S;* this *Qq.*

---

  99. S.D. *tucket*] flourish of trumpets.

That, staying them, we may confer and talk
With our brave prisoner and his double guard.—
Hieronimo, it greatly pleaseth us
That in our victory thou have a share, 125
By virtue of thy worthy son's exploit.
    Enter again.
Bring hither the young Prince of Portingale.
The rest march on; but, ere they be dismiss'd,
We will bestow on every soldier
Two ducats, and on every leader ten, 130
That they may know our largess welcomes them.
  Exeunt all [the Army] *but* Balthazar, Lorenzo, Horatio.
Welcome, Don Balthazar! welcome, nephew!
And thou, Horatio, thou art welcome too.
Young prince, although thy father's hard misdeeds,
In keeping back the tribute that he owes, 135
Deserve but evil measure at our hands,
Yet shalt thou know that Spain is honorable.
BALTHAZAR.
 The trespass that my father made in peace
Is now controll'd by fortune of the wars;
And cards once dealt, it boots not ask why so. 140
His men are slain—a weakening to his realm;
His colors seiz'd—a blot unto his name;
His son distress'd—a corsive to his heart:
These punishments may clear his late offence.
KING.
 Ay, Balthazar, if he observe this truce, 145
Our peace will grow the stronger for these wars.
Meanwhile live thou, though not in liberty,
Yet free from bearing any servile yoke;
For in our hearing thy deserts were great,
And in our sight thyself art gracious. 150
BALTHAZAR.
 And I shall study to deserve this grace.

129–131.] *M;* We ... ducats,/ And
... know/ Our ... them. *Qq.*

---

139. *controll'd*] checked.
143. *corsive*] corrosive; sharp or caustic medicine.

−67−

I.ii   THE SPANISH TRAGEDY

KING.
> But tell me—for their holding makes me doubt—
> To which of these twain art thou prisoner?

LORENZO.
> To me, my liege.

HORATIO.   To me, my sovereign.

LORENZO.
> This hand first took his courser by the reins.   155

HORATIO.
> But first my lance did put him from his horse.

LORENZO.
> I seiz'd his weapon, and enjoy'd it first.

HORATIO.
> But first I forc'd him lay his weapons down.

KING.
> Let go his arm, upon our privilege.   *Let him go.*
> Say, worthy prince, to whether didst thou yield?   160

BALTHAZAR.
> To him in courtesy, to this perforce.
> He spake me fair, this other gave me strokes;
> He promis'd life, this other threaten'd death;
> He wan my love, this other conquered me;
> And, truth to say, I yield myself to both.   165

HIERONIMO.
> But that I know your grace for just and wise,
> And might seem partial in this difference,
> Enforc'd by nature and by law of arms
> My tongue should plead for young Horatio's right.
> He hunted well that was a lion's death,   170
> Not he that in a garment wore his skin;
> So hares may pull dead lions by the beard.

KING.
> Content thee, Marshal, thou shalt have no wrong;

155. his] *Q1;* the *Q2–10.*   160. Say] *Q1;* So *Q2–10.*

---

159. *privilege*] royal prerogative.
160. *whether*] which of the two; cf. *1 Hieronimo,* xi.141.
164. *wan*] won.
167. *might*] that I might.
170–172.] Cf. Shakespeare, *King John,* II.i.137–138, 141–144; and Tilley, H 165.

—68—

THE SPANISH TRAGEDY   I.iii

    And, for thy sake, thy son shall want no right.
    Will both abide the censure of my doom?   175
LORENZO.
    I crave no better than your grace awards.
HORATIO.
    Nor I, although I sit beside my right.
KING.
    Then, by my judgment, thus your strife shall end:
    You both deserve, and both shall have reward.—
    Nephew, thou took'st his weapon and his horse;   180
    His weapons and his horse are thy reward.—
    Horatio, thou didst force him first to yield;
    His ransom therefore is thy valor's fee:
    Appoint the sum, as you shall both agree.—
    But nephew, thou shalt have the prince in guard, 185
    For thine estate best fitteth such a guest;
    Horatio's house were small for all his train.
    Yet, in regard thy substance passeth his,
    And that just guerdon may befall desert,
    To him we yield the armor of the prince.—   190
    How likes Don Balthazar of this device?
BALTHAZAR.
    Right well, my liege, if this proviso were,
    That Don Horatio bear us company,
    Whom I admire and love for chivalry.
KING.
    Horatio, leave him not that loves thee so.—   195
    Now let us hence to see our soldiers paid,
    And feast our prisoner as our friendly guest.   *Exeunt.*

[I.iii]   *Enter* Viceroy, Alexandro, Villuppo [, *Attendants*].
VICEROY.
    Is our ambassador despatch'd for Spain?
ALEXANDRO.
    Two days, my liege, are past since his depart.

177. sit] *Qq;* set *conj. E.*

---

  175. *censure*] opinion, judgment.
  177. *sit beside*] forgo.
  186. *estate*] social position.
  188. *passeth*] surpasses.

I.iii   THE SPANISH TRAGEDY

VICEROY.
    And tribute payment gone along with him?
ALEXANDRO.
    Ay, my good lord.
VICEROY.
    Then rest we here awhile in our unrest,   5
    And feed our sorrows with some inward sighs,
    For deepest cares break never into tears.
    But wherefore sit I in a regal throne?
    This better fits a wretch's endless moan.   *Falls to the ground.*
    Yet this is higher than my fortunes reach,   10
    And therefore better than my state deserves.
    Ay, ay, this earth, image of melancholy,
    Seeks him whom fates adjudge to misery.
    Here let me lie; now am I at the lowest.
    Qui jacet in terra, non habet unde cadat.   15
    In me consumpsit vires fortuna nocendo;
    Nil superest ut jam possit obesse magis.
    Yes, Fortune may bereave me of my crown:
    Here, take it now; let Fortune do her worst,
    She will not rob me of this sable weed: 20
    Oh no, she envies none but pleasant things:
    Such is the folly of despiteful chance.
    Fortune is blind, and sees not my deserts;
    So is she deaf, and hears not my laments;
    And could she hear, yet is she wilful-mad,   25
    And therefore will not pity my distress.
    Suppose that she could pity me, what then?
    What help can be expected at her hands
    Whose foot is standing on a rolling stone,
    And mind more mutable than fickle winds?   30
    Why wail I, then, where's hope of no redress?

9. S.D.] *Q9–10; after l. 11 in Q1–8.*
13. adjudge] *Q1;* adiuged *Q2–10.*
14. am I] *Q1–9;* I am *Q10.*
29. is] *D; not in Qq.*

15–17.] "He who lies on the ground, has nowhere to fall from; in hurting me Fortune has exhausted her power; nothing now remains that can harm me more."
    20. *weed*] garment.
    22. *despiteful*] spiteful, malicious.

Oh yes, complaining makes my grief seem less.
My late ambition hath distain'd my faith;
My breach of faith occasion'd bloody wars;
Those bloody wars have spent my treasure; 35
And with my treasure my people's blood;
And with their blood, my joy and best beloved,
My best beloved, my sweet and only son.
Oh, wherefore went I not to war myself?
The cause was mine; I might have died for both. 40
My years were mellow, his but young and green;
My death were natural, but his was forced.
ALEXANDRO.
No doubt, my liege, but still the prince survives.
VICEROY.
Survives! Ay, where?
ALEXANDRO.
In Spain, a prisoner by mischance of war. 45
VICEROY.
Then they have slain him for his father's fault.
ALEXANDRO.
That were a breach to common law of arms.
VICEROY.
They reck no laws that meditate revenge.
ALEXANDRO.
His ransom's worth will stay from foul revenge.
VICEROY.
No; if he lived, the news would soon be here. 50
ALEXANDRO.
Nay, evil news fly faster still than good.
VICEROY.
Tell me no more of news, for he is dead.
VILLUPPO.
My sovereign, pardon the author of ill news,
And I'll bewray the fortune of thy son.
VICEROY.
Speak on; I'll guerdon thee, whate'er it be. 55

---

33. *distain'd*] stained.
51. *still*] always.
54. *bewray*] reveal, betray.
55. *guerdon*] reward.

I.iii   THE SPANISH TRAGEDY

> Mine ear is ready to receive ill news,
> My heart grown hard 'gainst mischief's battery.
> Stand up, I say, and tell thy tale at large.

VILLUPPO.
> Then hear that truth which these mine eyes have seen.
> When both the armies were in battle join'd,   60
> Don Balthazar, amidst the thickest troops,
> To win renown did wondrous feats of arms.
> Amongst the rest, I saw him, hand to hand,
> In single fight with their lord general;
> Till Alexandro, that here counterfeits   65
> Under the color of a duteous friend,
> Discharged his pistol at the prince's back
> As though he would have slain their general;
> And therewithal Don Balthazar fell down;
> And when he fell, then we began to fly;   70
> But, had he lived, the day had sure been ours.

ALEXANDRO.
> Oh wicked forgery! Oh traitorous miscreant!

VICEROY.
> Hold thou thy peace!—But now, Villuppo, say,
> Where then became the carcass of my son?

VILLUPPO.
> I saw them drag it to the Spanish tents.   75

VICEROY.
> Ay, ay, my nightly dreams have told me this.—
> Thou false, unkind, unthankful, traitorous beast,
> Wherein had Balthazar offended thee,
> That thou shouldst thus betray him to our foes?
> Was't Spanish gold that bleared so thine eyes   80
> That thou couldst see no part of our deserts?
> Perchance, because thou art Terceira's lord,
> Thou hadst some hope to wear this diadem,

83. diadem] *Q 2–10* (Diademe);
Diadome *Q 1*.

---

58. *at large*] in full.
72. *forgery*] fabrication.
74. *Where then became*] what became of.
82. *Terceira*] one of the Azores, belonging to Portugal.

-72-

If first my son and then myself were slain;
But thy ambitious thought shall break thy neck. 85
Ay, this was it that made thee spill his blood;
Take the crown and put it on again.
But I'll now wear it till thy blood be spilt.
ALEXANDRO.
Vouchsafe, dread sovereign, to hear me speak.
VICEROY.
Away with him! His sight is second hell.
Keep him till we determine of his death.— 90
[*Exeunt Attendants with* Alexandro.]
If Balthazar be dead, he shall not live.
Villuppo, follow us for thy reward. *Exit* Viceroy.
VILLUPPO.
Thus have I with an envious, forged tale
Deceived the King, betray'd mine enemy,
And hope for guerdon of my villainy. *Exit.* 95

[I.iv] *Enter* Horatio *and* Bel-imperia.

BEL-IMPERIA.
Signior Horatio, this is the place and hour
Wherein I must entreat thee to relate
The circumstance of Don Andrea's death,
Who, living, was my garland's sweetest flower,
And in his death hath buried my delights. 5
HORATIO.
For love of him and service to yourself,
I nill refuse this heavy doleful charge;
Yet tears and sighs, I fear, will hinder me.
When both our armies were enjoin'd in fight,
Your worthy chevalier amidst the thick'st, 10
For glorious cause still aiming at the fairest,
Was at the last by young Don Balthazar
Encounter'd hand to hand. Their fight was long,

90.1] *E; not in Qq; They take him out. M.*

93. *envious*] malicious.
[I.iv]
7. *nill*] will not.

I.iv THE SPANISH TRAGEDY

Their hearts were great, their clamors menacing,
Their strength alike, their strokes both dangerous. 15
But wrathful Nemesis, that wicked power,
Envying at Andrea's praise and worth,
Cut short his life, to end his praise and worth.
She, she herself, disguis'd in armor's mask
(As Pallas was before proud Pergamus), 20
Brought in a fresh supply of halberdiers,
Which paunch'd his horse and ding'd him to the ground.
Then young Don Balthazar with ruthless rage,
Taking advantage of his foe's distress,
Did finish what his halberdiers begun, 25
And left not till Andrea's life was done.
Then, though too late, incens'd with just remorse,
I with my band set forth against the prince,
And brought him prisoner from his halberdiers.

BEL-IMPERIA.
Would thou hadst slain him that so slew my love! 30
But then was Don Andrea's carcass lost?

HORATIO.
No, that was it for which I chiefly strove;
Nor stepp'd I back till I recover'd him.
I took him up and wound him in mine arms,
And welding him unto my private tent, 35
There laid him down and dew'd him with my tears,
And sighed and sorrowed as became a friend.
But neither friendly sorrow, sighs, nor tears
Could win pale Death from his usurped right.
Yet this I did, and less I could not do: 40
I saw him honored with due funeral.
This scarf I pluck'd from off his lifeless arm,
And wear it in remembrance of my friend.

28. band] *Qq;* hand *B*.   38. sorrow] *Q 1–3;* sorrowes *Q 4–10.*

---

16. *Nemesis*] goddess of retribution.
20. *Pallas ... Pergamus*] Virgil *Aeneid* ii. 615–616.
22. *paunch'd*] stabbed in the belly.
22. *ding'd*] hurled.
27. *remorse*] regret, pity.
35. *welding*] carrying.

−74−

BEL-IMPERIA.
>I know the scarf; would he had kept it still!
>For had he lived, he would have kept it still, 45
>And worn it for his Bel-imperia's sake;
>For 'twas my favor at his last depart.
>But now wear thou it both for him and me;
>For after him thou hast deserved it best.
>But for thy kindness in his life and death, 50
>Be sure, while Bel-imperia's life endures,
>She will be Don Horatio's thankful friend.

HORATIO.
>And, madam, Don Horatio will not slack
>Humbly to serve fair Bel-imperia.
>But now, if your good liking stand thereto, 55
>I'll carve your pardon to go seek the prince;
>For so the duke, your father, gave me charge. *Exit.*

BEL-IMPERIA.
>Ay, go, Horatio; leave me here alone;
>For solitude best fits my cheerless mood.
>Yet what avails to wail Andrea's death, 60
>From whence Horatio proves my second love?
>Had he not loved Andrea as he did,
>He could not sit in Bel-imperia's thoughts.
>But how can love find harbor in my breast
>Till I revenge the death of my beloved? 65
>Yes, second love shall further my revenge:
>I'll love Horatio, my Andrea's friend,
>The more to spite the prince, that wrought his end.
>And where Don Balthazar, that slew my love,
>Himself now pleads for favor at my hands, 70
>He shall, in rigor of my just disdain,
>Reap long repentance for his murderous deed!
>For what was't else but murderous cowardice,
>So many to oppress one valiant knight,
>Without respect of honor in the fight? 75
>And here he comes that murder'd my delight.

Enter Lorenzo *and* Balthazar.

72. for] *Q1;* of *Q2–10.*

---

53. *slack*] be slow.

LORENZO.
Sister, what means this melancholy walk?
BEL-IMPERIA.
That for a while I wish no company.
LORENZO.
But here the prince is come to visit you.
BEL-IMPERIA.
That argues that he lives in liberty.   80
BALTHAZAR.
No, madam, but in pleasing servitude.
BEL-IMPERIA.
Your prison then, belike, is your conceit.
BALTHAZAR.
Ay, by conceit my freedom is enthrall'd.
BEL-IMPERIA.
Then with conceit enlarge yourself again.
BALTHAZAR.
What, if conceit have laid my heart to gage?   85
BEL-IMPERIA.
Pay that you borrowed, and recover it.
BALTHAZAR.
I die, if it return from whence it lies.
BEL-IMPERIA.
A heartless man, and live? A miracle!
BALTHAZAR.
Ay, lady, love can work such miracles.
LORENZO.
Tush, tush, my lord! let go these ambages,   90
And in plain terms acquaint her with your love.
BEL-IMPERIA.
What boots complaint, when there's no remedy?
BALTHAZAR.
Yes, to your gracious self must I complain,
In whose fair answer lies my remedy,
On whose perfection all my thoughts attend,   95

88. live] *Q1–3;* liues *Q4–10.*

82. *conceit*] imagination.
84. *enlarge*] set free.
85. *laid ... gage*] pledged, pawned my heart.
90. *ambages*] circumlocutions.

−76−

THE SPANISH TRAGEDY   I.iv

    On whose aspect mine eyes find beauty's bower,
    In whose translucent breast my heart is lodg'd.
BEL-IMPERIA.
    Alas, my lord, these are but words of course,
    And but device to drive me from this place.

She, in going in, lets fall her glove, which Horatio, *coming out, takes up.*
HORATIO.
    Madam, your glove.   100
BEL-IMPERIA.
    Thanks, good Horatio; take it for thy pains.
BALTHAZAR.
    Signior Horatio stoop'd in happy time.
HORATIO.
    I reap'd more grace than I deserv'd or hop'd.
LORENZO.
    My lord, be not dismay'd for what is past;
    You know that women oft are humorous.   105
    These clouds will overblow with little wind;
    Let me alone; I'll scatter them myself.
    Meanwhile, let us devise to spend the time
    In some delightful sports and revelling.
HORATIO.
    The king, my lords, is coming hither straight,   110
    To feast the Portingal ambassador;
    Things were in readiness before I came.
BALTHAZAR.
    Then here it fits us to attend the king,
    To welcome hither our ambassador,
    And learn my father and my country's health.   115

Enter the banquet, Trumpets, the King, [*Don Cyprian, Lords, Ladies,*] *and* Ambassador.

99. device] *Q 1–2* (deuise); deuisde *Q 3–10*.
99.1. in going] *Q 1*; going *Q 2–10*.
110. lords] *Q 1–2*; Lord *Q 3–10*.
111. Portingal] *Q 1–2*; Portugal *Q 3–10*.
115.1.] *Some edd. begin a new scene.*

---

  98. *words of course*] conventional phrases.
  99. *but device*] just a trick.
 105. *humorous*] capricious.
 107. *Let me alone*] Leave it to me.

–77–

I.iv   THE SPANISH TRAGEDY

KING.
   See, Lord Ambassador, how Spain entreats
   Their prisoner Balthazar, thy viceroy's son.
   We pleasure more in kindness than in wars.
AMBASSADOR.
   Sad is our king, and Portingale laments,
   Supposing that Don Balthazar is slain.   120
BALTHAZAR [*aside to* Bel-imperia].
   So am I slain, by beauty's tyranny!—
   You see, my lord, how Balthazar is slain:
   I frolic with the Duke of Castile's son,
   Wrapp'd every hour in pleasures of the court,
   And grac'd with favors of his majesty.   125
KING.
   Put off your greetings, till our feast be done;
   Now come and sit with us, and taste our cheer.
                                          Sit to the banquet.
   Sit down, young prince; you are our second guest.
   Brother, sit down; and, nephew, take your place.
   Signior Horatio, wait thou upon our cup;   130
   For well thou hast deserved to be honored.
   Now, lordings, fall to; Spain is Portugal,
   And Portugal is Spain; we both are friends;
   Tribute is paid, and we enjoy our right.
   But where is old Hieronimo, our marshal?   135
   He promised us, in honor of our guest,
   To grace our banquet with some pompous jest.

Enter Hieronimo, *with a Drum, three* Knights, *each his scutcheon; then he fetches three* Kings; *they take their crowns and them captive.*

   Hieronimo, this masque contents mine eye,
   Although I sound not well the mystery.

119. Portingale]   Q *1–2;*   Portugall
Q *3–10.*

---

116. *entreats*] treats.
137. *pompous*] stately.
137. *jest*] entertainment (=gest), masque.
137.1. *Drum*] drummer.
139. *sound . . . mystery*] do not fathom the underlying significance.

–78–

HIERONIMO.
 The first arm'd knight, that hung his scutcheon up,   140
   He takes the scutcheon and gives it to the King.
 Was English Robert, Earl of Gloucester,
 Who, when King Stephen bore sway in Albion,
 Arrived with five-and-twenty thousand men
 In Portingale, and by success of war
 Enforced the king, then but a Saracen,   145
 To bear the yoke of the English monarchy.

KING.
 My lord of Portingale, by this you see
 That which may comfort both your king and you,
 And make your late discomfort seem the less.—
 And say, Hieronimo, what was the next?   150

HIERONIMO.
 The second knight, that hung his scutcheon up,
   He doth as he did before.
 Was Edmund, Earl of Kent in Albion,
 When English Richard wore the diadem.
 He came likewise, and razed Lisbon walls,
 And took the King of Portingale in fight;   155
 For which and other suchlike service done,
 He after was created Duke of York.

KING.
 This is another special argument,
 That Portingale may deign to bear our yoke,
 When it by little England hath been yok'd.—   160
 But now, Hieronimo, what were the last?

HIERONIMO.
 The third and last, not least in our account,   *Doing as before.*
 Was, as the rest, a valiant Englishman,
 Brave John of Gaunt, the Duke of Lancaster,
 As by his scutcheon plainly may appear.   165
 He with a puissant army came to Spain
 And took our King of Castile prisoner.

AMBASSADOR.
 This is an argument for our viceroy

140–157.] a largely unhistorical account.

I.iv   THE SPANISH TRAGEDY

    That Spain may not insult for her success,
    Since English warriors likewise conquered Spain,   170
    And made them bow their knees to Albion.
KING.
    Hieronimo, I drink to thee for this device,
    Which hath pleas'd both the ambassador and me.
    Pledge me, Hieronimo, if thou love thy king.—
                                Takes the cup of Horatio.
    My lord, I fear we sit but overlong,   175
    Unless our dainties were more delicate;
    But welcome are you to the best we have.
    Now let us in, that you may be despatch'd;
    I think our council is already set.   *Exeunt omnes.*

[I.v]   [CHORUS]
ANDREA.
    Come we for this from depth of underground,
    To see him feast that gave me my death's wound?
    These pleasant sights are sorrow to my soul,
    Nothing but league, and love, and banqueting!
REVENGE.
    Be still, Andrea; ere we go from hence,   5
    I'll turn their friendship into fell despite,
    Their love to mortal hate, their day to night,
    Their hope into despair, their peace to war,
    Their joys to pain, their bliss to misery.

[II.i]   *Enter* Lorenzo *and* Balthazar.
LORENZO.
    My lord, though Bel-imperia seem thus coy,
    Let reason hold you in your wonted joy.
    In time the savage bull sustains the yoke,

174. thy] *S;* the *Qq.*

---

176. *Unless*] which would not be true if.
[I.v]
  6. *despite*] malice, ill will.
[II.i]
  1. *coy*] reluctant.
  2–10.] modeled on Watson's *Hecatompathia*, Sonnet 4.

In time all haggard hawks will stoop to lure,
In time small wedges cleave the hardest oak, 5
In time the flint is pierc'd with softest shower,
And she in time will fall from her disdain
And rue the sufferance of your friendly pain.

BALTHAZAR.
No, she is wilder, and more hard withal,
Than beast, or bird, or tree, or stony wall. 10
But wherefore blot I Bel-imperia's name?
It is my fault, not she, that merits blame.
My feature is not to content her sight;
My words are rude and work her no delight.
The lines I send her are but harsh and ill, 15
Such as do drop from Pan and Marsyas' quill.
My presents are not of sufficient cost,
And being worthless, all my labor's lost.
Yet might she love me for my valiancy—
Ay, but that's slander'd by captivity. 20
Yet might she love me to content her sire—
Ay, but her reason masters his desire.
Yet might she love me as her brother's friend—
Ay, but her hopes aim at some other end.
Yet might she love me to uprear her state— 25
Ay, but perhaps she hopes some nobler mate.
Yet might she love me as her beauty's thrall—
Ay, but I fear she cannot love at all.

LORENZO.
My lord, for my sake leave these ecstasies,
And doubt not but we'll find some remedy. 30

---

27. *beauty's*] *Q7–10;* beauteous *Q1–6;* duteous *conj. MSR.*

---

4. *haggard*] untamed.
4. *stoop to lure*] come down to the bait or food.
8. *sufferance*] patience in suffering.
12. *fault*] defect.
13. *feature*] form.
14. *rude*] rough, unpolished.
16. *Pan and Marsyas*] challenged by Apollo on the flute.
16. *quill*] reed.
20. *slander'd*] brought into disrepute.
29. *ecstasies*] frenzies.

II.i   THE SPANISH TRAGEDY

    Some cause there is that lets you not be loved;
    First that must needs be known, and then removed.
    What if my sister love some other knight?

BALTHAZAR.
    My summer's day will turn to winter's night.

LORENZO.
    I have already found a stratagem   35
    To sound the bottom of this doubtful theme.
    My lord, for once you shall be rul'd by me;
    Hinder me not, whate'er you hear or see.
    By force or fair means will I cast about
    To find the truth of all this question out.—   40
    Ho, Pedringano!

PEDRINGANO.   *Signior!*
LORENZO.   *Vien qui presto.*

Enter Pedringano.

PEDRINGANO.
    Hath your lordship any service to command me?

LORENZO.
    Ay, Pedringano, service of import;
    And, not to spend the time in trifling words,
    Thus stands the case: It is not long, thou know'st,   45
    Since I did shield thee from my father's wrath,
    For thy conveyance in Andrea's love,
    For which thou wert adjudg'd to punishment.
    I stood betwixt thee and thy punishment;
    And since, thou knowest how I have favored thee.   50
    Now to these favors will I add reward,
    Not with fair words, but store of golden coin,
    And lands and living join'd with dignities,
    If thou but satisfy my just demand.
    Tell truth, and have me for thy lasting friend.   55

PEDRINGANO.
    Whate'er it be your lordship shall demand,

---

41. *qui*] *C;* que *Qq*.   53. living] *Q1–3;* liuings *Q4–10*.

  41. *Vien qui presto*] Come here quickly.
  47. *conveyance*] acting as go-between; secret agency.

My bounden duty bids me tell the truth,
If case it lie in me to tell the truth.
LORENZO.
   Then, Pedringano, this is my demand:
   Whom loves my sister Bel-imperia? 60
   For she reposeth all her trust in thee.
   Speak, man, and gain both friendship and reward.
   I mean, whom loves she in Andrea's place?
PEDRINGANO.
   Alas, my lord, since Don Andrea's death
   I have no credit with her as before, 65
   And therefore know not if she love or no.
LORENZO.
   Nay, if thou dally, then I am thy foe; [*Draw his sword.*]
   And fear shall force what friendship cannot win.
   Thy death shall bury what thy life conceals;
   Thou diest for more esteeming her than me. 70
PEDRINGANO.
   Oh, stay, my lord!
LORENZO.
   Yet speak the truth, and I will guerdon thee,
   And shield thee from whatever can ensue,
   And will conceal whate'er proceeds from thee;
   But if thou dally once again, thou diest. 75
PEDRINGANO.
   If Madam Bel-imperia be in love—
LORENZO.
   What villain!—if's and and's? [*Offer to kill him.*]
PEDRINGANO.
   Oh, stay, my lord! she loves Horatio.   Balthazar *starts back.*
LORENZO.
   What, Don Horatio, our Knight Marshal's son?
PEDRINGANO.
   Even him, my lord. 80
LORENZO.
   Now say but how knowest thou he is her love,

67. S.D.] *Q 4–10; not in Q 1–3.*   81. say] *D;* say, *Qq.*
77. S.D.] *Q 4–10; not in Q 1–3.*

58. *If case*] supposing.

−83−

And thou shalt find me kind and liberal.
Stand up, I say, and fearless tell the truth.
PEDRINGANO.
She sent him letters, which myself perus'd,
Full-fraught with lines and arguments of love, 85
Preferring him before Prince Balthazar.
LORENZO.
Swear on this cross that what thou sayest is true,
And that thou wilt conceal what thou hast told.
PEDRINGANO.
I swear to both, by Him that made us all.
LORENZO.
In hope thine oath is true, here's thy reward; 90
But if I prove thee perjur'd and unjust,
This very sword whereon thou took'st thine oath
Shall be the worker of thy tragedy.
PEDRINGANO.
What I have said is true, and shall, for me,
Be still conceal'd from Bel-imperia. 95
Besides, your honor's liberality
Deserves my duteous service, even till death.
LORENZO.
Let this be all that thou shalt do for me:
Be watchful when and where these lovers meet,
And give me notice in some secret sort. 100
PEDRINGANO.
I will, my lord.
LORENZO.
Then shalt thou find that I am liberal.
Thou know'st that I can more advance thy state
Than she; be therefore wise, and fail me not.
Go and attend her, as thy custom is, 105
Lest absence make her think thou dost amiss. *Exit* Pedringano.
Why so! *Tam armis quam ingenio*:
Where words prevail not, violence prevails;
But gold doth more than either of them both.
How likes Prince Balthazar this stratagem? 110

---

87. *this cross*] his sword-hilt.
107. *Tam ... ingenio*] as much by force as by ingenuity.

BALTHAZAR.
   Both well and ill; it makes me glad and sad:
   Glad, that I know the hinderer of my love,
   Sad, that I fear she hates me whom I love;
   Glad, that I know on whom to be reveng'd,
   Sad, that she'll fly me if I take revenge.   115
   Yet must I take revenge, or die myself,
   For love resisted grows impatient.
   I think Horatio be my destin'd plague!
   First, in his hand he brandished a sword,
   And with that sword he fiercely waged war,   120
   And in that war he gave me dangerous wounds,
   And by those wounds he forced me to yield,
   And by my yielding I became his slave;
   Now in his mouth he carries pleasing words,
   Which pleasing words do harbor sweet conceits,   125
   Which sweet conceits are lim'd with sly deceits,
   Which sly deceits smooth Bel-imperia's ears,
   And through her ears dive down into her heart,
   And in her heart set him where I should stand.
   Thus hath he ta'en my body by his force,   130
   And now by sleight would captivate my soul;
   But in his fall I'll tempt the Destinies,
   And either lose my life or win my love.
LORENZO.
   Let's go, my lord; your staying stays revenge.
   Do you but follow me, and gain your love;   135
   Her favor must be won by his remove.   *Exeunt.*

[II.ii]   *Enter* Horatio *and* Bel-imperia.

HORATIO.
   Now, madam, since by favor of your love
   Our hidden smoke is turn'd to open flame,
   And that with looks and words we feed our thoughts
   (Two chief contents, where more cannot be had);

---

  126. *lim'd*] made to snare, as birds with birdlime.
  127. *smooth*] flatter, humor.
[II.ii]
  3. *that*] since.

II.ii   THE SPANISH TRAGEDY

                Thus, in the midst of love's fair blandishments,   5
                Why show you sign of inward languishments?

Pedringano showeth all to the Prince and Lorenzo, placing them in secret [above].

BEL-IMPERIA.
                My heart, sweet friend, is like a ship at sea:
                She wisheth port, where, riding all at ease,
                She may repair what stormy times have worn,
                And, leaning on the shore, may sing with joy   10
                That pleasure follows pain, and bliss annoy.
                Possession of thy love is th'only port
                Wherein my heart, with fears and hopes long toss'd,
                Each hour doth wish and long to make resort,
                There to repair the joys that it hath lost,   15
                And, sitting safe, to sing in Cupid's choir
                That sweetest bliss is crown of love's desire.

                Balthazar [and Lorenzo speak] above.

BALTHAZAR.
                Oh sleep, mine eyes: see not my love profan'd;
                Be deaf, my ears: hear not my discontent;
                Die, heart: another joys what thou deservest.   20
LORENZO.
                Watch still, mine eyes, to see this love disjoin'd;
                Hear still, mine ears, to hear them both lament;
                Live, heart, to joy at fond Horatio's fall.
BEL-IMPERIA.
                Why stands Horatio speechless all this while?
HORATIO.
                The less I speak, the more I meditate.   25
BEL-IMPERIA.
                But whereon dost thou chiefly meditate?
HORATIO.
                On dangers past, and pleasures to ensue.

6.2. above] *E; not in Qq.*   *Q1–4;* Balthazar *and* Lorenzo *alone*
9. may] *Q4–10;* mad *Q1;* made   *Q5–10.*
Q2–3.   19. my ears] *Q1–6;* mine ears
17.1.] *this edn.;* Balthazar aboue   *Q7–10.*

        6.1–2] See Introduction, p. xx.
        23. *fond*] foolish.

                            –86–

BALTHAZAR.
>   On pleasures past, and dangers to ensue.

BEL-IMPERIA.
>   What dangers and what pleasures dost thou mean?

HORATIO.
>   Dangers of war, and pleasures of our love.   30

LORENZO.
>   Dangers of death, but pleasures none at all.

BEL-IMPERIA.
>   Let dangers go; thy war shall be with me,
>   But such a war as breaks no bond of peace.
>   Speak thou fair words, I'll cross them with fair words;
>   Send thou sweet looks, I'll meet them with sweet looks;   35
>   Write loving lines, I'll answer loving lines;
>   Give me a kiss, I'll countercheck thy kiss:
>   Be this our warring peace, or peaceful war.

HORATIO.
>   But, gracious madam, then appoint the field
>   Where trial of this war shall first be made.   40

BALTHAZAR.
>   Ambitious villain, how his boldness grows!

BEL-IMPERIA.
>   Then be thy father's pleasant bower the field,
>   Where first we vow'd a mutual amity.
>   The court were dangerous; that place is safe.
>   Our hour shall be when Vesper 'gins to rise,   45
>   That summons home distressful travelers.
>   There none shall hear us but the harmless birds;
>   Happily the gentle nightingale
>   Shall carol us asleep, ere we be 'ware,
>   And, singing with the prickle at her breast,   50
>   Tell our delight and mirthful dalliance.
>   Till then each hour will seem a year and more.

33. war] *D, S;* warring *Qq.*

---

42. *bower*] the "arbor" of II.iv.53.1.
45. *Vesper*] the evening star.
46. *distressful*] exhausted with toil.
46. *travelers*] travailers; laborers.
48. *Happily*] haply, perhaps.
50. *prickle*] thorn: to keep her awake and complaining, as in legend.

II.ii   THE SPANISH TRAGEDY

HORATIO.
> But, honey-sweet and honorable love,
> Return we now into your father's sight;
> Dangerous suspicion waits on our delight.   55

LORENZO.
> Ay, danger mix'd with jealous despite
> Shall send thy soul into eternal night.   *Exeunt.*

[II.iii]
Enter King of Spain, Portingale Ambassador, Don Cyprian [Duke of Castile], *etc.*

KING.
> Brother of Castile, to the prince's love
> What says your daughter, Bel-imperia?

CASTILE.
> Although she coy it, as becomes her kind,
> And yet dissemble that she loves the prince,
> I doubt not, I, but she will stoop in time.   5
> And were she froward, which she will not be,
> Yet herein shall she follow my advice,
> Which is to love him, or forgo my love.

KING.
> Then, Lord Ambassador of Portingale,
> Advise thy king to make this marriage up,   10
> For strengthening of our late-confirmed league:
> I know no better means to make us friends.
> Her dowry shall be large and liberal;
> Besides that she is daughter and half-heir
> Unto our brother here, Don Cyprian,   15
> And shall enjoy the moiety of his land,
> I'll grace her marriage with an uncle's gift;
> And this it is, in case the match go forward:
> The tribute which you pay shall be releas'd;

56. jealous] *S;* iealous *Qq*.   [II.iii]
                                        0.1,2. Duke of Castile] *edd.; not in Q*.

---

   56. *jealious*] jealous (trisyllabic).
[II.iii]
    3. *coy it*] affect shyness.
    3. *her kind*] womankind.
   16. *moiety*] half.

And if by Balthazar she have a son, 20
He shall enjoy the kingdom after us.
AMBASSADOR.
I'll make the motion to my sovereign liege,
And work it, if my counsel may prevail.
KING.
Do so, my lord; and, if he give consent,
I hope his presence here will honor us, 25
In celebration of the nuptial day;
And let himself determine of the time.
AMBASSADOR.
Will't please your grace command me aught beside?
KING.
Commend me to the king, and so farewell.
But where's Prince Balthazar to take his leave? 30
AMBASSADOR.
That is perform'd already, my good lord.
KING.
Amongst the rest of what you have in charge,
The prince's ransom must not be forgot.
That's none of mine, but his that took him prisoner;
And well his forwardness deserves reward. 35
It was Horatio, our Knight Marshal's son.
AMBASSADOR.
Between us there's a price already pitch'd,
And shall be sent with all convenient speed.
KING.
Then once again farewell, my lord.
AMBASSADOR.
Farewell, my lord of Castile, and the rest. *Exit.* 40
KING.
Now, brother, you must take some little pains
To win fair Bel-imperia from her will.
Young virgins must be ruled by their friends.
The prince is amiable, and loves her well;
If she neglect him and forgo his love, 45
She both will wrong her own estate and ours.

---

37. *pitch'd*] settled, agreed.
42. *will*] wilfulness.

II.iii   THE SPANISH TRAGEDY

    Therefore, whiles I do entertain the prince
    With greatest pleasure that our court affords,
    Endeavor you to win your daughter's thought:
    If she give back, all this will come to naught.   *Exeunt.*   50

[II.iv]   *Enter* Horatio, Bel-imperia, *and* Pedringano.

HORATIO.
    Now that the night begins with sable wings
    To overcloud the brightness of the sun,
    And that in darkness pleasures may be done,
    Come, Bel-imperia, let us to the bower,
    And there in safety pass a pleasant hour.   5
BEL-IMPERIA.
    I follow thee, my love, and will not back,
    Although my fainting heart controls my soul.
HORATIO.
    Why, make you doubt of Pedringano's faith?
BEL-IMPERIA.
    No, he is as trusty as my second self.—
    Go, Pedringano, watch without the gate,   10
    And let us know if any make approach.
PEDRINGANO [*aside*].
    Instead of watching, I'll deserve more gold
    By fetching Don Lorenzo to this match.   *Exit* Pedringano.
HORATIO.
    What means my love?
BEL-IMPERIA.   I know not what myself;
    And yet my heart foretells me some mischance.   15
HORATIO.
    Sweet, say not so; fair Fortune is our friend,
    And heavens have shut up day to pleasure us.
    The stars, thou seest, hold back their twinkling shine,
    And Luna hides herself to pleasure us.

49. thought]   *Q7–10;*   thoughts   *Q1–6.*

---

  50. *give back*] turn her back on us; reject us.
[II.iv]
    7. *controls*] overpowers.
    10. *without*] outside.

BEL-IMPERIA.
>   Thou hast prevail'd; I'll conquer my misdoubt,   20
>   And in thy love and counsel drown my fear.
>   I fear no more; love now is all my thoughts.
>   Why sit we not? for pleasure asketh ease.

HORATIO.
>   The more thou sitt'st within these leavy bowers,
>   The more will Flora deck it with her flowers.   25

BEL-IMPERIA.
>   Ay, but if Flora spy Horatio here,
>   Her jealous eye will think I sit too near.

HORATIO.
>   Hark, madam, how the birds record by night,
>   For joy that Bel-imperia sits in sight.

BEL-IMPERIA.
>   No, Cupid counterfeits the nightingale,   30
>   To frame sweet music to Horatio's tale.

HORATIO.
>   If Cupid sing, then Venus is not far;
>   Ay, thou art Venus, or some fairer star.

BEL-IMPERIA.
>   If I be Venus, thou must needs be Mars;
>   And where Mars reigneth, there must needs be wars.   35

HORATIO.
>   Then thus begin our wars: put forth thy hand,
>   That it may combat with my ruder hand.

BEL-IMPERIA.
>   Set forth thy foot to try the push of mine.

HORATIO.
>   But first my looks shall combat against thine.

BEL-IMPERIA.
>   Then ward thyself: I dart this kiss at thee.   40

HORATIO.
>   Thus I retort the dart thou threw'st at me.

BEL-IMPERIA.
>   Nay, then, to gain the glory of the field,

35. wars] *D;* warre *Qq.*

---

20. *misdoubt*] mistrust, suspicion.
28. *record*] sing, repeat their songs.
41. *retort*] hurl back.

II.iv   THE SPANISH TRAGEDY

    My twining arms shall yoke and make thee yield.
HORATIO.
    Nay, then, my arms are large and strong withal:
    Thus elms by vines are compass'd, till they fall.   45
BEL-IMPERIA.
    Oh, let me go, for in my troubled eyes
    Now may'st thou read that life in passion dies.
HORATIO.
    Oh, stay awhile, and I will die with thee;
    So shalt thou yield, and yet have conquer'd me.
BEL-IMPERIA.
    Who's there? Pedringano! We are betray'd!   50

Enter Lorenzo, Balthazar, Serberine, [*and*] Pedringano, *disguised.*

LORENZO.
    My lord, away with her; take her aside.—
    Oh, sir, forbear; your valor is already tried.
    Quickly dispatch, my masters.

                  They hang him in the arbor.

HORATIO.
    What, will you murder me?
LORENZO.
    Ay, thus, and thus! These are the fruits of love.   55
                                          They stab him.
BEL-IMPERIA.
    Oh, save his life, and let me die for him!
    Oh, save him, brother; save him, Balthazar!
    I loved Horatio but he loved not me.
BALTHAZAR.
    But Balthazar loves Bel-imperia.
LORENZO.
    Although his life were still ambitious-proud,   60
    Yet is he at the highest now he is dead.

---

50. Who's there? Pedringano!] *S;*   Who's there? Pedringano? *Hz.*
Whose there Pedringano? *Qq;*

---

    44. *withal*] in addition, as well.
    47, 48. *dies ... die*] for the double sense, cf. Shakespeare, *Romeo and Juliet,* V.iii.120, and *Othello,* V.ii.359.

—92—

BEL-IMPERIA.
Murder! murder! Help, Hieronimo, help!
LORENZO.
Come, stop her mouth; away with her.   *Exeunt.*

[II.v]   Enter Hieronimo *in his shirt, etc.*

HIERONIMO.
What outcries pluck me from my naked bed,
And chill my throbbing heart with trembling fear,
Which never danger yet could daunt before?
Who calls Hieronimo? Speak, here I am.—
I did not slumber; therefore 'twas no dream.   5
No, no, it was some woman cried for help,
And here within this garden did she cry,
And in this garden must I rescue her.—
But stay, what murd'rous spectacle is this?
A man hang'd up and all the murderers gone!   10
And in my bower, to lay the guilt on me!
This place was made for pleasure, not for death.
                                    He cuts him down.
Those garments that he wears I oft have seen—
Alas, it is Horatio, my sweet son!
Oh no, but he that whilom was my son!   15
Oh, was it thou that call'dst me from my bed?
Oh speak, if any spark of life remain!
I am thy father. Who hath slain my son?
What savage monster, not of human kind,
Hath here been glutted with thy harmless blood,   20
And left thy bloody corpse dishonored here,
For me, amidst this dark and deathful shades,
To drown thee with an ocean of my tears?
Oh heavens, why made you night to cover sin?
By day this deed of darkness had not been.   25
Oh earth, why didst thou not in time devour
The vile profaner of this sacred bower?
Oh poor Horatio, what hadst thou misdone,
To leese thy life, ere life was new begun?

---

15. *whilom*] formerly.
29. *leese*] lose.

II.v   THE SPANISH TRAGEDY

    Oh wicked butcher, whatsoe'er thou wert,   30
    How could thou strangle virtue and desert?
    Ay me most wretched, that have lost my joy,
    In leesing my Horatio, my sweet boy!

          Enter Isabella.

ISABELLA.
    My husband's absence makes my heart to throb!—
    Hieronimo!   35
HIERONIMO.
    Here, Isabella, help me to lament;
    For sighs are stopp'd, and all my tears are spent.
ISABELLA.
    What world of grief— my son, Horatio!
    Oh, where's the author of this endless woe?
HIERONIMO.
    To know the author were some ease of grief,   40
    For in revenge my heart would find relief.
ISABELLA.
    Then is he gone? And is my son gone too?
    Oh, gush out, tears, fountains and floods of tears;
    Blow, sighs, and raise an everlasting storm;
    For outrage fits our cursed wretchedness.   45

        [*First passage of additions.*]

    [Ay me, Hieronimo, sweet husband, speak!
HIERONIMO.
    He supp'd with us tonight, frolic and merry,
    And said he would go visit Balthazar
    At the duke's palace; there the prince doth lodge.
    He had no custom to stay out so late;   (*50*)
    He may be in his chamber; some go see.
    Roderigo, ho!

        Enter Pedro *and* Jaques

ISABELLA.
    Ay me, he raves! —Sweet Hieronimo!
HIERONIMO.
    True, all Spain takes note of it.

31. could] *Q1-3;* could'st *Q4-10.*

---

45. *outrage*] uncontrolled outcry.

THE SPANISH TRAGEDY   II.v

    Besides, he is so generally beloved;   (55)
    His majesty the other day did grace him
    With waiting on his cup: these be favors
    Which do assure he cannot be short-lived.
ISABELLA.
    Sweet Hieronimo!
HIERONIMO.
    I wonder how this fellow got his clothes!—   (60)
    Sirrah, sirrah, I'll know the truth of all!—
    Jaques, run to the Duke of Castile's presently,
    And bid my son Horatio to come home.
    I and his mother have had strange dreams tonight.
    Do ye hear me, sir?
JAQUES.   Ay, sir.
HIERONIMO.   Well, sir, begone.—   (65)
    Pedro, come hither; knowest thou who this is?
PEDRO.
    Too well, sir.
HIERONIMO.
    Too well! Who, who is it? —Peace, Isabella!—
    Nay, blush not, man.
PEDRO.   It is my lord Horatio.
HIERONIMO.
    Ha, ha, St. James! but this doth make me laugh,   (70)
    That there are more deluded than myself.
PEDRO.
    Deluded?
HIERONIMO.   Ay!
    I would have sworn, myself, within this hour,
    That this had been my son Horatio—
    His garments are so like. Ha! are they not great
        persuasions?   (75)
ISABELLA.
    Oh, would to God it were not so!
HIERONIMO.
    Were not, Isabella? Dost thou dream it is?

(*58*). he] *E;* me *Q4, 6;* me he
Q5, 7; me that he *Q8-10.*

  (*58*). *assure*] guarantee.
  (*75*). *persuasions*] evidence.

II.v   THE SPANISH TRAGEDY

        Can thy soft bosom entertain a thought
        That such a black deed of mischief should be done
        On one so pure and spotless as our son?   (80)
        Away, I am ashamed.
ISABELLA.   Dear Hieronimo,
        Cast a more serious eye upon thy grief;
        Weak apprehension gives but weak belief.
HIERONIMO.
        It was a man, sure, that was hanged up here;
        A youth, as I remember: I cut him down.   (85)
        If it should prove my son, now after all!
        Say you? say you? —Light! Lend me a taper;
        Let me look again. —Oh God!
        Confusion, mischief, torment, death, and hell,
        Drop all your stings at once in my cold bosom,   (90)
        That now is stiff with horror; kill me quickly!
        Be gracious to me, thou infective night,
        And drop this deed of murder down on me;
        Gird in my waste of grief with thy large darkness,
        And let me not survive to see the light   (95)
        May put me in the mind I had a son.
ISABELLA.
        Oh sweet Horatio! Oh my dearest son!
HIERONIMO.
        How strangely had I lost my way to grief!]
        Sweet, lovely rose, ill-pluck'd before thy time,   46   (99)
        Fair, worthy son, not conquer'd, but betray'd,
        I'll kiss thee now, for words with tears are stay'd.
ISABELLA.
        And I'll close up the glasses of his sight,
        For once these eyes were only my delight.   50   (103)
HIERONIMO.
        Seest thou this handkercher besmear'd with blood?

(80). pure] Q 7–10; poore Q 4–6.   48. stay'd] Q 5–10 (staide); stainde
                                  Q 1–4.

---

   (83). *apprehension*] understanding, intelligence.
   (92). *infective*] infectious.
     46. *Sweet, lovely rose*] Cf. Shakespeare, *1 Henry IV*, I.iii.175, and Kyd's
Soliman and Perseda, V.iv.81.
     49. *glasses of his sight*] Cf. Shakespeare, *Coriolanus*, III.ii.118.

It shall not from me till I take revenge.
Seest thou those wounds that yet are bleeding fresh?
I'll not entomb them till I have reveng'd.
Then will I joy amidst my discontent; 55 *(108)*
Till then my sorrow never shall be spent.

ISABELLA.
The heavens are just; murder cannot be hid;
Time is the author both of truth and right,
And time will bring this treachery to light.

HIERONIMO.
Meanwhile, good Isabella, cease thy plaints, 60 *(113)*
Or, at the least, dissemble them awhile;
So shall we sooner find the practice out,
And learn by whom all this was brought about.
Come, Isabel, now let us take him up, *They take him up.*
And bear him in from out this cursed place. 65 *(118)*
I'll say his dirge; singing fits not this case.
O aliquis mihi quas pulchrum ver educat herbas,

Hieronimo sets his breast unto his sword.

Misceat, et nostro detur medicina dolori;
Aut, si qui faciunt animis oblivia, succos
Praebeat; ipse metam magnum quaecunque per orbem 70 *(123)*

54. reveng'd] *Q 1–8;* revenge *Q 9–10.*
67. ver] *Q 2–10;* var *Q 1.*
67. educat] *Q 7–10;* educet *Q 1–6.*
69. animis] *E;* annum *Qq;* annorum *Hw.*
69. oblivia] *Hw;* oblimia *Qq.*
70. metam] *Hw;* metum *Qq.*
70. magnum] *Q 2–8;* magnam *Q 1, 9–10.*
70. quaecunque] *Hw;* quicunque *Qq.*

---

62. *practice*] plot.
67–80.] "May someone mix for me the herbs that the beautiful spring brings forth, and medicine be administered to our grief; or let him furnish juices, if such there be, that will bring oblivion to our minds. May I myself reap throughout the wide world whatever the sun brings forth into the lovely realms of light. May I myself drink whatever poison the wise woman may contrive, and also whatever herbs the goddess weaves by her occult power; may I seek out everything, even death, if once for all every feeling may die in my dead heart. So, my life, shall I never more see your eyes. And has eternal sleep buried your light? May I die with you—thus, thus it is pleasing to go to the shades. Nevertheless I shall abstain from yielding to a speedy death, lest then no vengeance would follow your death." The passage is a mixture of classical fragments with Kyd's own invention.

II.v   THE SPANISH TRAGEDY

    Gramina Sol pulchras effert in luminis oras;
    Ipse bibam quicquid meditatur saga veneni,
    Quicquid et herbarum vi caeca nenia nectit:
    Omnia perpetiar, lethum quoque, dum semel omnis
    Noster in extincto moriatur pectore sensus.—   75   (*128*)
    Ergo tuos oculos nunquam, mea vita, videbo,
    Et tua perpetuus sepelivit lumina somnus?
    Emoriar tecum: sic, sic, juvat ire sub umbras.—
    At tamen absistam properato cedere letho,
    Ne mortem vindicta tuam tam nulla sequatur.   80   (*133*)

        Here he throws it from him and bears the body away.

[II.vi]   [CHORUS]

ANDREA.
    Brought'st thou me hither to increase my pain?
    I look'd that Balthazar should have been slain;
    But 'tis my friend Horatio that is slain,
    And they abuse fair Bel-imperia,
    On whom I doted more than all the world,   5
    Because she lov'd me more than all the world.
REVENGE.
    Thou talkest of harvest, when the corn is green;
    The end is crown of every work well done;
    The sickle comes not till the corn be ripe.
    Be still; and ere I lead thee from this place,   10
    I'll show thee Balthazar in heavy case.

[III.i]   *Enter* Viceroy of Portingale, Nobles, Villuppo.

VICEROY.
    Infortunate condition of kings,
    Seated amidst so many helpless doubts!
    First we are plac'd upon extremest height,

---

71. *effert ... oras*] S; *effecit ... oras*   *nenia* Hw; *irraui euecaeca menia* Qq.
Qq; *ejecit lucis in oras* Hw.   [III.i]
72. *veneni*] Q2–10; *veneri* Q1.   0.1. Nobles, Villuppo.] *edd.*; Nobles
73. *herbarum ... nenia*] S; *irarum ...*   Alexandro, Villuppo. Qq.

---

  8. *The ... crown*] a familiar Latin saying, *Finis coronat opus.*
[III.i]
  1–11.] adapted from Seneca *Agamemnon* 57–73 (B).

-98-

THE SPANISH TRAGEDY   III.i

 And oft supplanted with exceeding hate,
 But ever subject to the whèel of chance;   5
 And at our highest never joy we so
 As we both doubt and dread our overthrow.
 So striveth not the waves with sundry winds
 As Fortune toileth in the affairs of kings,
 That would be fear'd, yet fear to be beloved, 10
 Sith fear or love to kings is flattery:
 For instance, lordings, look upon your king,
 By hate deprived of his dearest son,
 The only hope of our successive line.
NOBLEMAN.
 I had not thought that Alexandro's heart   15
 Had been envenom'd with such extreme hate;
 But now I see that words have several works,
 And there's no credit in the countenance.
VILLUPPO.
 No; for, my lord, had you beheld the train
 That feigned love had colored in his looks,   20
 When he in camp consorted Balthazar,
 Far more inconstant had you thought the sun,
 That hourly coasts the center of the earth,
 Than Alexandro's purpose to the prince.
VICEROY.
 No more, Villuppo; thou hast said enough;   25
 And with thy words thou slay'st our wounded thoughts.
 Nor shall I longer dally with the world,
 Procrastinating Alexandro's death.—
 Go some of you, and fetch the traitor forth,
         [*Exit a* Nobleman.]
 That, as he is condemned, he may die.   30

  Enter Alexandro *with a* Nobleman *and* Halberts.

4. hate] *Q 3–10, edd.;* heat *Q 1–2.* 26. slay'st] *Qq;* staiest *B.*

---

7. *doubt*] fear, suspect.
11. *Sith*] since.
17. *several works*] various outcome in deeds.
18.] Cf. Shakespeare, *Macbeth*, I.iv.11–12.
19–20. *train/ That . . . had colored*] treachery . . . posing as (love).
21. *consorted*] kept company with.
23. *coasts . . . earth*] moves round this center, the earth.
30.1. *Halberts*] halberdiers.

III.i   THE SPANISH TRAGEDY

NOBLEMAN.
    In such extremes will nought but patience serve.
ALEXANDRO.
    But in extremes what patience shall I use?
    Nor discontents it me to leave the world,
    With whom there nothing can prevail but wrong.
NOBLEMAN.
    Yet hope the best.
ALEXANDRO.   'Tis heaven is my hope.   35
    As for the earth, it is too much infect
    To yield me hope of any of her mold.
VICEROY.
    Why linger ye? Bring forth that daring fiend,
    And let him die for his accursed deed.
ALEXANDRO.
    Not that I fear the extremity of death—   40
    For nobles cannot stoop to servile fear—
    Do I, oh king, thus discontented live.
    But this, oh this, torments my laboring soul,
    That thus I die suspected of a sin
    Whereof, as heavens have known my secret thoughts,   45
    So am I free from this suggestion.
VICEROY.
    No more, I say! To the tortures! When!
    Bind him, and burn his body in those flames
                              They bind him to the stake.
    That shall prefigure those unquenched fires
    Of Phlegethon, prepared for his soul.   50
ALEXANDRO.
    My guiltless death will be aveng'd on thee,
    On thee, Villuppo, that hath malic'd thus,
    Or for thy meed hast falsely me accus'd.
VILLUPPO.
    Nay, Alexandro, if thou menace me,
    I'll lend a hand to send thee to the lake   55

---

    36. *infect*] infected, corrupt.
    46. *suggestion*] false accusation or representation.
    47. *When!*] an exclamation of impatience.
    50. *Phlegethon*] a fabled river of fire in the underworld; cf. l. 55.
    52. *malic'd*] entertained or shown malice.

Where those thy words shall perish with thy works,
Injurious traitor! Monstrous homicide!

Enter Ambassador.

AMBASSADOR.
   Stay, hold a while;
   And here—with pardon of his majesty—
   Lay hands upon Villuppo.
VICEROY.   Ambassador,   60
   What news hath urg'd this sudden entrance?
AMBASSADOR.
   Know, sovereign lord, that Balthazar doth live.
VICEROY.
   What sayst thou? Liveth Balthazar, our son?
AMBASSADOR.
   Your highness' son, Lord Balthazar, doth live;
   And, well entreated in the court of Spain,   65
   Humbly commends him to your majesty.
   These eyes beheld, and these my followers;
   With these, the letters of the king's commends, *Gives him letters.*
   Are happy witness of his highness' health.

   The King *looks on the letters, and proceeds.*

VICEROY.
   "Thy son doth live; your tribute is receiv'd;   70
   Thy peace is made, and we are satisfied.
   The rest resolve upon as things propos'd
   For both our honors and thy benefit."
AMBASSADOR.
   These are his highness' farther articles. *He gives him more letters.*
VICEROY.
   Accursed wretch, to intimate these ills   75
   Against the life and reputation
   Of noble Alexandro! —Come, my lord,

69. witness] *Q 8–10;* witnesses *Q 1–7,*   77. lord] *E;* lord, vnbinde him: *Qq. S, B.*

---

   57. *Injurious*] calumnious.
   57. *Monstrous*] unnatural, like a monster.
   65. *entreated*] treated, entertained.
   68. *commends*] commendations, greetings.

III.i   THE SPANISH TRAGEDY

    Let him unbind thee, that is bound to death,
    To make a quital for thy discontent.   *They unbind him.*

ALEXANDRO.
    Dread lord, in kindness you could do no less   80
    Upon report of such a damned fact;
    But thus we see our innocence hath sav'd
    The hopeless life which thou, Villuppo, sought
    By thy suggestions to have massacred.

VICEROY.
    Say, false Villuppo, wherefore didst thou thus   85
    Falsely betray Lord Alexandro's life?
    Him whom thou knowest that no unkindness else,
    But even the slaughter of our dearest son,
    Could once have moved us to have misconceived.

ALEXANDRO.
    Say, treacherous Villuppo, tell the king: 90
    Wherein hath Alexandro used thee ill?

VILLUPPO.
    Rent with remembrance of so foul a deed,
    My guilty soul submits me to thy doom;
    For, not for Alexandro's injuries,
    But for reward and hope to be preferr'd,   95
    Thus have I shameless hazarded his life.

VICEROY.
    Which, villain, shall be ransomed with thy death;
    And not so mean a torment as we here
    Devis'd for him who, thou said'st, slew our son,
    But with the bitterest torments and extremes   100
    That may be yet invented for thine end.
                           Alexandro seems to entreat.
    Entreat me not. —Go, take the traitor hence.—
                              Exit Villuppo [*guarded*].

91. Wherein] *Hz;* Or wherein *Qq.*   96. shameless] *this edn.;* shamelessly *Qq.*

---

  79. *quital*] requital.
  80. *kindness*] nature.
  81. *fact*] deed.
  87. *unkindness*] unnatural deed.
  95. *preferr'd*] promoted, favored.
  98. *mean*] moderate—as opposed to "extremes" (l. 100).

And, Alexandro, let us honor thee
With public notice of thy loyalty.—
To end those things articulated here 105
By our great lord, the mighty King of Spain,
We with our council will deliberate.
Come, Alexandro, keep us company. *Exeunt.*

[III.ii] *Enter* Hieronimo.

HIERONIMO.
Oh eyes! no eyes, but fountains fraught with tears;
Oh life! no life, but lively form of death;
Oh world! no world, but mass of public wrongs,
Confus'd and fill'd with murder and misdeeds.
Oh sacred heavens! if this unhallowed deed, 5
If this inhuman, barbarous attempt,
If this incomparable murder thus
Of mine, but now no more my son,
Shall unreveal'd and unrevenged pass,
How should we term your dealings to be just, 10
If you unjustly deal with those that in your justice trust?
The night, sad secretary to my moans,
With direful visions wake my vexed soul,
And with the wounds of my distressful son
Solicit me for notice of his death. 15
The ugly fiends do sally forth of hell,
And frame my steps to unfrequented paths,
And fear my heart with fierce inflamed thoughts.
The cloudy day my discontents records,
Early begins to register my dreams, 20
And drive me forth to seek the murderer.
Eyes, life, world, heavens, hell, night, and day,

---

6. *inhuman*] *this edn.;* inhuman and   11. *those that in*] *Qq; those conj.*
Qq.   *this edn.*

---

105. *articulated*] set forth in articles.
[III.ii]
  1–4.] a passage often imitated or parodied.
  2. *lively*] lifelike.   12. *secretary*] confidant.
  13, 15, 21. *wake . . . Solicit . . . drive*] probably attracted into the singular by "moans" (l. 12).
  14. *distressful*] unfortunate; causing great distress.
  18. *fear*] frighten.

III.ii   THE SPANISH TRAGEDY

See, search, show, send some man, some mean, that may—
A letter falleth.
What's here? A letter? Tush! it is not so!—
A letter written to Hieronimo!—   *Red ink.*   25
"For want of ink, receive this bloody writ.
Me hath my hapless brother hid from thee;
Revenge thyself on Balthazar and him:
For these were they that murdered thy son.
Hieronimo, revenge Horatio's death,   30
And better fare than Bel-imperia doth."—
What means this unexpected miracle?
My son slain by Lorenzo and the prince!
What cause had they Horatio to malign?
Or what might move thee, Bel-imperia,   35
To accuse thy brother, had he been the mean?
Hieronimo, beware!—thou art betray'd,
And to entrap thy life this train is laid.
Advise thee, therefore; be not credulous:
This is devised to endanger thee,   40
That thou, by this, Lorenzo shouldst accuse;
And he, for thy dishonor done, should draw
Thy life in question and thy name in hate.
Dear was the life of my beloved son,
And of his death behoves me be reveng'd.   45
Then hazard not thine own, Hieronimo,
But live t'effect thy resolution.
I therefore will by circumstances try,
What I can gather to confirm this writ;
And, heark'ning near the Duke of Castile's house,   50
Close, if I can, with Bel-imperia,
To listen more, but nothing to bewray.

Enter Pedringano.

Now, Pedringano!

26. For] *edd.*; *Bel.* For *Qq.*   32. What] *edd.*; *Hiero.* What *Qq.*
29. murdered] *edd.*; murdred *Qq.*

---

25. S.D. *Red ink*] to represent blood—probably a note by the author or prompter.
34. *malign*] hate.
38. *train*] trap.
48. *circumstances*] circumstantial evidence (E).

-104-

THE SPANISH TRAGEDY   III.ii

PEDRINGANO.   Now, Hieronimo!
HIERONIMO.
   Where's thy lady?
PEDRINGANO.   I know not; here's my lord.

                  Enter Lorenzo.

LORENZO.
   How now, who's this? Hieronimo?
HIERONIMO.   My lord.   55
PEDRINGANO.
   He asketh for my Lady Bel-imperia.
LORENZO.
   What to do, Hieronimo? The duke, my father, hath
   On some disgrace awhile remov'd her hence;
   But, if it be aught I may inform her of,
   Tell me, Hieronimo, and I'll let her know it.   60
HIERONIMO.
   Nay, nay, my lord, I thank you, it shall not need.
   I had a suit unto her, but too late,
   And her disgrace makes me unfortunate.
LORENZO.
   Why so, Hieronimo; use me.
HIERONIMO.
   Oh no, my lord, I dare not; it must not be.   65
   I humbly thank your lordship.

              [*Second passage of additions.*]

[HIERONIMO.
   Who, you, my lord?   (65)
   I reserve your favor for a greater honor;
   This is a very toy, my lord, a toy.
LORENZO.
   All's one, Hieronimo; acquaint me with it.
HIERONIMO.
   I'faith, my lord, it is an idle thing;

58. On] *this edn.;* Vpon *Qq.*   *first part of 66 in Q 1–4.*
(65)–(74). HIERONIMO. Who . . .   (69). it is] *S;* 'tis *Qq.*
   lord!] *Q 4–10, replacing lines 65 and*

   (67). *toy*] trifle.

                      −105−

III.ii   THE SPANISH TRAGEDY

      I must confess I ha' been too slack, too tardy,   (70)
      Too remiss unto your honor.
LORENZO.   How now, Hieronimo?
HIERONIMO.
      In troth, my lord, it is a thing of nothing:
      The murder of a son, or so—
      A thing of nothing, my lord!]
LORENZO.   Why then, farewell.   66   (74)
HIERONIMO.
      My grief no heart, my thoughts no tongue can tell.   *Exit.*
LORENZO.
      Come hither, Pedringano; seest thou this?
PEDRINGANO.
      My lord, I see it, and suspect it too.
LORENZO.
      This is that damned villain, Serberine,   70   (78)
      That hath, I fear, reveal'd Horatio's death.
PEDRINGANO.
      My lord, he could not, 'twas so lately done;
      And since, he hath not left my company.
LOREZNO.
      Admit he have not, his condition's such
      As fear or flattering words may make him false.   75   (83)
      I know his humor, and therewith repent
      That e'er I us'd him in this enterprise.
      But, Pedringano, to prevent the worst,
      And 'cause I know thee secret as my soul,
      Here, for thy further satisfaction, take thou this,   80   (88)
                                     Gives him more gold.
      And hearken to me: thus it is devis'd:
      This night thou must (and, prithee, so resolve),
      Meet Serberine at Saint Luigi's Park—
      Thou knowest 'tis here hard by behind the house—
      There take thy stand, and see thou strike him sure,   85   (93)
      For die he must, if we do mean to live.
PEDRINGANO.
      But how shall Serberine be there, my lord?

---

(72). *of nothing*] of no importance.
74. *condition*] nature.
78. *prevent*] anticipate.

THE SPANISH TRAGEDY   III.ii

LORENZO.
    Let me alone; I'll send to him to meet
    The prince and me, where thou must do this deed.
PEDRINGANO.
    It shall be done, my lord; it shall be done;   90 (*98*)
    And I'll go arm myself to meet him there.
LORENZO.
    When things shall alter, as I hope they will,
    Then shalt thou mount for this; thou knowest my mind.
                                        Exit Pedringano.
  Che le Ieron!

                Enter Page.

PAGE.   My lord?
LORENZO.   Go, sirrah,
    To Serberine, and bid him forthwith meet   95 (*103*)
    The prince and me at Saint Luigi's Park
    Behind the house; this evening, boy!
PAGE.   I go, my lord.
LORENZO.
    But, sirrah, let the hour be eight o'clock:
    Bid him not fail.
PAGE.   I fly, my lord.   *Exit.*
LORENZO.
    Now to confirm the complot thou hast cast   100 (*108*)
    Of all these practices, I'll spread the watch,
    Upon precise commandment from the king,
    Strongly to guard the place where Pedringano
    This night shall murder hapless Serberine.
    Thus must we work that will avoid distrust;   105 (*113*)
    Thus must we practice to prevent mishap,
    And thus one ill another must expulse.

98. S.P. LORENZO.] *Q4–10; not in
Q1–3.*

---

  88. *Let me alone*] leave that to me.
  93. *mount*] (*a*) by promotion; (*b*) by hanging; cf. II.iv.61, and see III.v–vi.
  94. *Che le Ieron!*] "An unintelligible expression, possibly a corruption of the page's name" (B).
  100. *complot*] plot.
  100. *cast*] planned.
  101. *practices*] schemes.

III.ii   THE SPANISH TRAGEDY

    This sly enquiry of Hieronimo
    For Bel-imperia breeds suspicion,
    And this suspicion bodes a further ill.   110   (*118*)
    As for myself, I know my secret fault,
    And so do they; but I have dealt for them.
    They that for coin their souls endangered,
    To save my life, for coin shall venture theirs;
    And better 'tis that base companions die   115   (*123*)
    Than by their life to hazard our good haps.
    Nor shall they live, for me to fear their faith:
    I'll trust myself, myself shall be my friend;
    Slaves are ordained to no other end.   *Exit.*

[III.iii]   *Enter* Pedringano *with a pistol.*

PEDRINGANO.
    Now, Pedringano, bid thy pistol hold;
    And hold on, Fortune! once more favor me;
    Give but success to mine attempting spirit,
    And let me shift for taking of mine aim!
    Here is the gold: this is the gold propos'd;   5
    It is no dream that I adventure for,
    But Pedringano is possess'd thereof.
    And he that would not strain his conscience
    For him that thus his liberal purse hath stretch'd,
    Unworthy such a favor, may he fail,   10
    And, wishing, want, when such as I prevail.
    As for the fear of apprehension,
    I know, if need should be, my noble lord
    Will stand between me and ensuing harms;
    Besides, this place is free from all suspect.   15
    Here therefore will I stay and take my stand.

115. 'tis] *Q 3–10;* its *Q 1–2.*   *Qq.*
119.] *this edn.;* For dye they shall, [III.iii]
slaues . . . end. *Qq.*   1. S.P. PEDRINGANO] *edd.; not in*
119. ordained] *this edn.;* ordeind   *Qq.*

    111. *fault*] offence.
    115. *base companions*] fellows of mean rank.
[III.iii]
    4. *let . . . for*] I'll attend to.
    15. *suspect*] suspicion.

THE SPANISH TRAGEDY   III.iii

Enter the Watch.

1.
    I wonder much to what intent it is
    That we are thus expressly charg'd to watch.
2.
    'Tis by commandment in the king's own name.
3.
    But we were never wont to watch and ward   20
    So near the duke his brother's house before.
2.
    Content yourself; stand close; there's somewhat in't.

Enter Serberine.

SERBERINE.
    Here, Serberine, attend and stay thy pace;
    For here did Don Lorenzo's page appoint
    That thou by his command shouldst meet with him.   25
    How fit a place, if one were so dispos'd,
    Methinks this corner is to close with one.
PEDRINGANO.
    Here comes the bird that I must seize upon.
    Now, Pedringano, or never, play the man!
SERBERINE.
    I wonder that his lordship stays so long,   30
    Or wherefore should he send for me so late.
PEDRINGANO.
    For this, Serberine; and thou shalt ha't.   *Shoots the dag.*
    So, there he lies; my promise is perform'd.

The Watch.

1.
    Hark, gentlemen, this is a pistol shot.
2.
    And here's one slain—stay the murderer.   35
PEDRINGANO.
    Now by the sorrows of the souls in hell,
                   He strives with the Watch.

---

  20. *watch and ward*] keep guard.
  22. *close*] out of sight.
  22. *somewhat in't*] something going on.
  23. *attend*] wait.
  32. S.D. *dag*] pistol.

III.iii   THE SPANISH TRAGEDY

  Who first lays hand on me, I'll be his priest.
3.
  Sirrah, confess, and therein play the priest;
  Why hast thou thus unkindly kill'd the man?
PEDRINGANO.
  Why? Because he walk'd abroad so late.   40
3.
  Come, sir, you had been better kept your bed,
  Than have committed this misdeed so late.
2.
  Come, to the Marshal's with the murderer.
1.
  On to Hieronimo's! Help me here
  To bring the murder'd body with us too.   45
PEDRINGANO.
  Hieronimo? Carry me before whom you will.
  Whate'er he be, I'll answer him and you;
  And do your worst, for I defy you all.   *Exeunt.*

[III.iv]   *Enter* Lorenzo *and* Balthazar.
BALTHAZAR.
  How now, my lord, what makes you rise so soon?
LORENZO.
  Fear of preventing our mishaps too late.
BALTHAZAR.
  What mischief is it that we not mistrust?
LORENZO.
  Our greatest ills we least mistrust, my lord,
  And inexpected harms do hurt us most.   5
BALTHAZAR.
  Why, tell me, Don Lorenzo, tell me, man,
  If aught concerns our honor and your own.
LORENZO.
  Nor you, nor me, my lord, but both in one;
  For I suspect—and the presumption's great—

---

 37. *be his priest*] see him to the next world; kill him.
 39. *unkindly*] unnaturally.
 40. *abroad*] outside; from home.
[III.iv]
 3. *mischief*] evil, misfortune.
 3. *mistrust*] suspect the existence of.

That by those base confederates in our fault 10
Touching the death of Don Horatio,
We are betray'd to old Hieronimo.

BALTHAZAR.
Betray'd, Lorenzo? Tush! it cannot be.

LORENZO.
A guilty conscience, urged with the thought
Of former evils, easily cannot err. 15
I am persuaded, and dissuade me not,
That all's revealed to Hieronimo.
And therefore know that I have cast it thus—
[*Enter* Page.]
But here's the page. How now? What news with thee?

PAGE.
My lord, Serberine is slain. 20

BALTHAZAR.
Who? Serberine, my man?

PAGE.
Your highness' man, my lord.

LORENZO.
Speak, page, who murdered him?

PAGE.
He that is apprehended for the fact.

LORENZO.
Who? 25

PAGE.
Pedringano.

BALTHAZAR.
Is Serberine slain, that lov'd his lord so well?
Injurious villain, murderer of his friend!

LORENZO.
Hath Pedringano murdered Serberine?
My lord, let me entreat you take the pains 30
To exasperate and hasten his revenge
With your complaints unto my lord the king.
This their dissension breeds a greater doubt.

---

30. take] *this edn.;* to take *Qq.*

31. *exasperate*] make rough or harsh.
31. *his*] upon him.

III.iv   THE SPANISH TRAGEDY

BALTHAZAR.
    Assure thee, Don Lorenzo, he shall die,
    Or else his highness hardly shall deny.   35
    Meanwhile I'll haste the marshal-sessions,
    For die he shall for this his damned deed.   *Exit* Balthazar.

LORENZO.
    Why, so; this fits our former policy,
    And thus experience bids the wise to deal.
    I lay the plot; he prosecutes the point.   40
    I set the trap; he breaks the worthless twigs,
    And sees not that wherewith the bird was lim'd.
    Thus hopeful men, that mean to hold their own,
    Must look like fowlers to their dearest friends.
    He runs to kill whom I have holp to catch,   45
    And no man knows it was my reaching fatch.
    'Tis hard to trust unto a multitude,
    Or any one, in mine opinion,
    When men themselves their secrets will reveal.—

              Enter a Messenger *with a letter.*
    Boy!   50

PAGE.
    My lord.

LORENZO.
    What's he?

MESSENGER.   I have a letter to your lordship.

LORENZO.
    From whence?

MESSENGER.   From Pedringano, that's imprisoned.

LORENZO.
    So he is in prison, then?

MESSENGER.   Ay, my good lord.

LORENZO.
    What would he with us? —He writes us here,   55
    To stand good lord, and help him in distress.—
    Tell him I have his letters, know his mind;
    And what we may, let him assure him of.
    Fellow, begone; my boy shall follow thee.—   *Exit* Messenger.

---

    35. *hardly shall deny*] shall show harshness in denying me (E).
    45. *holp*] helped.
    46. *reaching fatch*] far-reaching fetch or stratagem.
    56. *stand good lord*] act as his protector.

This works like wax; yet once more try thy wits.— 60
Boy, go, convey this purse to Pedringano;
Thou knowest the prison; closely give it him,
And be advis'd that none be thereabout.
Bid him be merry still, but secret;
And though the marshal-sessions be today, 65
Bid him not doubt of his delivery.
Tell him his pardon is already sign'd,
And thereon bid him boldly be resolved;
For, were he ready to be turned off—
As 'tis my will the uttermost be tried— 70
Thou with his pardon shalt attend him still.
Show him this box, tell him his pardon's in't;
But open't not, and if thou lovest thy life;
But let him wisely keep his hopes unknown:
He shall not want while Don Lorenzo lives. 75
Away!

PAGE.   I go, my lord, I run.
LORENZO.
But, sirrah, see that this be cleanly done.— *Exit* Page.
Now stands our fortune on a tickle point,
And now or never ends Lorenzo's doubts.
One only thing is uneffected yet, 80
And that's to see the executioner.
But to what end? I list not trust the air
With utterance of our pretense therein,
For fear the privy whisp'ring of the wind
Convey our words amongst unfriendly ears, 85
That lie too open to advantages.
E quel che voglio io, nessun lo sa;
Intendo io: quel mi basterà. *Exit.*

87. *E*] edd.; *Et Qq.*   87. *lo*] edd.; *le Qq.*
87. *io*] edd.; *Ii Q1; Il Q2–10.*   88. *basterà*] *S; bassara Qq.*

---

69. *turned off*] hanged.
73. *and if*] if.
77. *cleanly*] efficiently.
78. *tickle*] ticklish, critical.
82. *list not*] do not choose or like.
83. *pretense*] intention.
87–88.] "And what I wish, no one knows; I understand; that will be enough for me."

III.v   THE SPANISH TRAGEDY

[III.v]   *Enter* Boy *with the box.*

BOY.
    My master hath forbidden me to look in this box; and, by my
troth, 'tis likely, if he had not warned me, I should not have
had so much idle time; for we men's-kind in our minority
are like women in their uncertainty: that they are most for-
bidden, they will soonest attempt. So I now. —By my bare   5
honesty, here's nothing but the bare empty box! Were it
not sin against secrecy, I would say it were a piece of
gentlemanlike knavery. I must go to Pedringano, and tell
him his pardon is in this box; nay, I would have sworn it,
had I not seen the contrary. I cannot choose but smile to   10
think how the villain will flout the gallows, scorn the
audience, and descant on the hangman, and all presuming of
his pardon from hence. Will't not be an odd jest for me to
stand and grace every jest he makes, pointing my finger at
this box, as who would say, "Mock on; here's thy warrant."   15
Is't not a scurvy jest that a man should jest himself to death?
Alas! poor Pedringano, I am in a sort sorry for thee; but if
I should be hanged with thee, I cannot weep.   *Exit.*

[III.vi]   *Enter* Hieronimo *and the* Deputy.

HIERONIMO.
    Thus must we toil in other men's extremes,
That know not how to remedy our own,
And do them justice, when unjustly we,
For all our wrongs, can compass no redress.
But shall I never live to see the day.   5
That I may come, by justice of the heavens,
To know the cause that may my cares allay?
This toils my body, this consumeth age,
That only I to all men just must be,
And neither gods nor men be just to me.   10
DEPUTY.
    Worthy Hieronimo, your office asks
A care to punish such as do transgress.

[III.vi]
    0.1. *Deputy*] assistant (to Hieronimo).

THE SPANISH TRAGEDY   III.vi

HIERONIMO.
    So is't my duty to regard his death
    Who, when he lived, deserved my dearest blood.
    But come, for that we came for. Let's begin,   15
    For here lies that which bids me to be gone.

Enter Officers, Boy, *and* Pedringano, *with a letter in his hand, bound.*

DEPUTY.
    Bring forth the prisoner, for the court is set.
PEDRINGANO.
    Gramercy, boy, but it was time to come;
    For I had written to my lord anew
    A nearer matter that concerneth him,   20
    For fear his lordship had forgotten me.
    But sith he hath remember'd me so well—
    Come, come, come on, when shall we to this gear?
HIERONIMO.
    Stand forth, thou monster, murderer of men,
    And here, for satisfaction of the world,   25
    Confess thy folly, and repent thy fault;
    For there's thy place of execution.
PEDRINGANO.
    This is short work. Well, to your marshalship
    First I confess, nor fear I death therefore,
    I am the man, 'twas I slew Serberine.   30
    But, sir, then you think this shall be the place
    Where we shall satisfy you for this gear?
DEPUTY.
    Ay, Pedringano.
PEDRINGANO.   Now I think not so.
HIERONIMO.
    Peace, impudent; for thou shalt find it so;
    For blood with blood shall, while I sit as judge,   35
    Be satisfied, and the law discharg'd.
    And though myself cannot receive the like,

---

  13. *regard*] have regard or concern for.
  16. *here*] in his heart or head (E); referring to the bloody kercher (handkerchief) (B).
  23. *gear*] business.

—115—

III.vi   The Spanish Tragedy

Yet will I see that others have their right.
Despatch; the fault's approved and confess'd,
And by our law he is condemn'd to die.   40

HANGMAN.
    Come on, sir; are you ready?
PEDRINGANO.
    To do what, my fine, officious knave?
HANGMAN.
    To go to this gear.
PEDRINGANO.
    Oh sir, you are too forward: thou wouldst fain furnish me with a halter, to disfurnish me of my habit. So I should go   45 out of this gear, my raiment, into that gear, the rope. But, hangman, now I spy your knavery, I'll not change without boot, that's flat.
HANGMAN.
    Come, sir.
PEDRINGANO.
    So, then, I must up?   50
HANGMAN.
    No remedy.
PEDRINGANO.
    Yes, but there shall be for my coming down.
HANGMAN.
    Indeed, here's a remedy for that.
PEDRINGANO.
    How? be turn'd off?
HANGMAN.
    Ay, truly. Come, are you ready? I pray, sir, dispatch; the   55 day goes away.
PEDRINGANO.
    What, do you hang by the hour? If you do, I may chance to break your old custom.
HANGMAN.
    Faith, you have reason; for I am like to break your young neck.   60

---

39. *approved*] proved.
45. *habit*] clothes (which would go to the hangman).
48. *boot*] compensation.

−116−

PEDRINGANO.
>   Dost thou mock me, hangman? Pray God, I be not preserved to break your knave's pate for this!

HANGMAN.
>   Alas, sir, you are a foot too low to reach it, and I hope you will never grow so high while I am in the office.

PEDRINGANO.
>   Sirrah, dost see yonder boy with the box in his hand?   65

HANGMAN.
>   What, he that points to it with his finger?

PEDRINGANO.
>   Ay, that companion.

HANGMAN.
>   I know him not; but what of him?

PEDRINGANO.
>   Dost thou think to live till his old doublet will make thee a new truss?   70

HANGMAN.
>   Ay, and many a fair year after, to truss up many an honester man than either thou or he.

PEDRINGANO.
>   What hath he in his box, as thou think'st?

HANGMAN.
>   Faith, I cannot tell, nor I care not greatly. Methinks you should rather hearken to your soul's health.   75

PEDRINGANO.
>   Why, sirrah hangman, I take it that that is good for the body is likewise good for the soul; and it may be in that box is balm for both.

HANGMAN.
>   Well, thou art even the merriest piece of man's flesh that e'er groan'd at my office door.   80

PEDRINGANO.
>   Is your roguery become an office with a knave's name?

HANGMAN.
>   Ay, and that shall all they witness that see you seal it with a thief's name.

---

69. *doublet*] waistcoat.
70, 71. *truss*] (*a*) close-fitting jacket; (*b*) hang.

III.vi   The Spanish Tragedy

PEDRINGANO.
> I prithee, request this good company to pray with me.

HANGMAN.
> Ay, marry, sir, this is a good motion. My masters, you see   85
> here's a good fellow.

PEDRINGANO.
> Nay, nay, now I remember me, let them alone till some
> other time; for now I have no great need.

HIERONIMO.
> I have not seen a wretch so impudent.
> Oh monstrous times, where murder's set so light,   90
> And where the soul, that should be shrin'd in heaven,
> Solely delights in interdicted things,
> Still wand'ring in the thorny passages
> That intercepts itself of happiness.
> Murder! Oh bloody monster! God forbid   95
> A fault so foul should scape unpunished.
> Dispatch, and see this execution done!—
> This makes me to remember thee, my son.   *Exit* Hieronimo.

PEDRINGANO.
> Nay, soft, no haste.

DEPUTY.
> Why, wherefore stay you? Have you hope of life?   100

PEDRINGANO.
> Why, ay.

HANGMAN.
> As how?

PEDRINGANO.
> Why, rascal, by my pardon from the king.

HANGMAN.
> Stand you on that? Then you shall off with this.
>   *He turns him off.*

DEPUTY.
> So, executioner; convey him hence;   105
> But let his body be unburied:
> Let not the earth be choked or infect
> With that which heaven contemns, and men neglect.
>   *Exeunt.*

108. heaven] *Q2–10;* heauens *Q1.*

---

85. *motion*] proposal.

[III.vii] *Enter* Hieronimo.

HIERONIMO.
Where shall I run to breathe abroad my woes,
My woes, whose weight hath wearied the earth?
Or mine exclaims, that have surcharged the air
With ceaseless plaints for my deceased son?
The blust'ring winds, conspiring with my words,   5
At my lament have moved the leaveless trees,
Disrob'd the meadows of their flower'd green,
Made mountains marsh with spring-tides of my tears,
And broken through the brazen gates of hell.
Yet still tormented is my tortured soul   10
With broken sighs and restless passions,
That, winged, mount and, hovering in the air,
Beat at the windows of the brightest heavens,
Soliciting for justice and revenge:
But they are plac'd in those empyreal heights,   15
Where, countermur'd with walls of diamond,
I find the place impregnable; and they
Resist my woes, and give my words no way.

Enter Hangman *with a letter.*

HANGMAN.
Oh Lord, sir! God bless you, sir! the man, sir, Petergade,
sir, he that was so full of merry conceits—   20
HIERONIMO.
Well, what of him?
HANGMAN.
Oh Lord, sir, he went the wrong way; the fellow had a fair
commission to the contrary. Sir, here is his passport; I pray
you, sir, we have done him wrong.
HIERONIMO.
I warrant thee; give it me.   25
HANGMAN.
You will stand between the gallows and me?
HIERONIMO.
Ay, ay.

---

16. *countermur'd*] doubly walled.
20. *conceits*] far-fetched ideas or fanciful phrases.

III.vii   THE SPANISH TRAGEDY

HANGMAN.
    I thank your lord worship.   *Exit* Hangman.
HIERONIMO.
    And yet, though somewhat nearer me concerns,
    I will, to ease the grief that I sustain,   30
    Take truce with sorrow while I read on this.
    "My lord, I writ as mine extremes requir'd,
    That you would labor my delivery;
    If you neglect, my life is desperate,
    And in my death I shall reveal the troth.   35
    You know, my lord, I slew him for your sake;
    And as confederate with the prince and you,
    Won by rewards and hopeful promises,
    I holp to murder Don Horatio too."—
    Holp he to murder mine Horatio?   40
    And actors in th'accursed tragedy
    Wast thou, Lorenzo, Balthazar and thou,
    Of whom my son, my son, deserved so well?
    What have I heard, what have mine eyes beheld?
    Oh sacred heavens, may it come to pass   45
    That such a monstrous and detested deed,
    So closely smother'd, and so long conceal'd,
    Shall thus by this be venged or reveal'd?
    Now see I what I durst not then suspect,
    That Bel-imperia's letter was not feign'd.   50
    Nor feigned she, though falsely they have wrong'd
    Both her, myself, Horatio, and themselves.
    Now may I make compare 'twixt hers and this,
    Of every accident; I ne'er could find
    Till now, and now I feelingly perceive   55
    They did what heaven unpunish'd would not leave.
    Oh false Lorenzo, are these thy flattering looks?
    Is this the honor that thou didst my son?
    And Balthazar—bane to thy soul and me—
    Was this the ransom he reserv'd thee for?   60
    Woe to the cause of these constrained wars!
    Woe to thy baseness and captivity!

32. writ] *M;* write *Qq.*   37. as] *E;* was *Qq.*

54. *accident*] circumstance.

Woe to thy birth, thy body and thy soul,
Thy cursed father, and thy conquer'd self!
And bann'd with bitter execrations be 65
The day and place where he did pity thee!
But wherefore waste I mine unfruitful words,
When naught but blood will satisfy my woes?
I will go plain me to my lord the king,
And cry aloud for justice through the court, 70
Wearing the flints with these my withered feet,
And either purchase justice by entreats,
Or tire them all with my revenging threats. *Exit.*

[III.viii] *Enter* Isabella *and her* Maid.

ISABELLA.
So that you say this herb will purge the eye,
And this, the head?
Ah, but none of them will purge the heart.
No, there's no medicine left for my disease,
Nor any physic to recure the dead. *She runs lunatic.* 5
Horatio! Oh, where's Horatio?

MAID.
Good madam, affright not thus yourself
With outrage for your son Horatio:
He sleeps in quiet in the Elysian fields.

ISABELLA.
Did I not give you gowns and goodly things, 10
Bought you a whistle and a whipstalk too.
To be revenged on their villainies?

MAID.
Madam, these humors do torment my soul.

---

10. Did] *this edn.;* Why, did *Qq.*

---

65. *bann'd*] cursed.
69. *plain me*] complain.
72. *purchase*] obtain otherwise than by inheritance.
[III.viii]
   5. *recure*] recover.
   8. *outrage*] outcry, passion.
  11. *whipstalk*] whipstock, handle of a whip.
  13. *humors*] extravagant fancies.

−121−

III.viii   THE SPANISH TRAGEDY

ISABELLA.
    "My soul"—poor soul, thou talks of things
    Thou know'st not what—my soul hath silver wings,   15
    That mounts me up unto the highest heavens.
    To heaven! Ay, there sits my Horatio,
    Back'd with a troop of fiery cherubins,
    Dancing about his newly-healed wounds,
    Singing sweet hymns and chanting heavenly notes,   20
    Rare harmony to greet his innocence,
    That died, ay, died, a mirror in our days.
    But say, where shall I find the men, the murderers,
    That slew Horatio? Whither shall I run
    To find them out that murdered my son?   *Exeunt.*   25

[III.ix]   Bel-imperia. *at a window.*

BEL-IMPERIA.
    What means this outrage that is offer'd me?
    Why am I thus sequester'd from the court?
    No notice! Shall I not know the cause
    Of these my secret and suspicious ills?
    Accursed brother, unkind murderer,   5
    Why bends thou thus thy mind to martyr me?
    Hieronimo, why writ I of thy wrongs,
    Or why art thou so slack in thy revenge?
    Andrea, oh Andrea! that thou sawest
    Me for thy friend Horatio handled thus,   10
    And him for me thus causeless murdered!—
    Well, force perforce, I must constrain myself
    To patience, and apply me to the time,
    Till heaven, as I have hoped, shall set me free.

               Enter Christophil.

CHRISTOPHIL.
    Come, Madam Bel-imperia, this may not be.   *Exeunt.*   15

14. talks] *Q 1–8;* talk'st *Q 9–10.*   [III.ix]
                                    6. bends] *Q 1–8;* bend'st *Q 9–10.*

[III.ix]
   2. *sequester'd*] kept apart.
   3. *notice*] information.
   13. *apply . . . time*] conform to the present situation.

[III.x]   *Enter* Lorenzo, Balthazar, *and the* Page.

LORENZO.
  Boy, talk no further; thus far things go well.
  Thou art assur'd that thou sawest him dead?
PAGE.
  Or else, my lord, I live not.
LORENZO.   That's enough.
  As for his resolution in his end,
  Leave that to Him with whom he sojourns now.   5
  Here, take my ring and give it Christophil,
  And bid him let my sister be enlarg'd,
  And bring her hither straight.—   *Exit* Page.
  This that I did was for a policy,
  To smooth and keep the murder secret,   10
  Which, as a nine-days' wonder, being o'er-blown,
  My gentle sister will I now enlarge.
BALTHAZAR.
  And time, Lorenzo; for my lord the duke,
  You heard, inquired for her yesternight.
LORENZO.
  Why, and, my lord, I hope you heard me say   15
  Sufficient reason why she kept away;
  But that's all one. My lord, you love her?
BALTHAZAR.   Ay.
LORENZO.
  Then in your love beware; deal cunningly;
  Salve all suspicions; only soothe me up;
  And if she hap to stand on terms with us,   20
  As for her sweetheart, and concealment so,
  Jest with her gently: under feigned jest
  Are things conceal'd that else would breed unrest.
  But here she comes.
            Enter Bel-imperia.
            Now, sister—
BEL-IMPERIA.   Sister? No!

---

  7. *enlarg'd*] set free.   9. *policy*] stratagem, plan.
  12. *gentle*] noble.   19. *Salve*] smooth over.
  19. *soothe me up*] corroborate what I say.
  20. *stand on terms*] make conditions, be difficult.

–123–

|||||||Thou art no brother, but an enemy; 25
Else wouldst thou not have us'd thy sister so:
First, to affright me with thy weapons drawn,
And with extremes abuse my company;
And then to hurry me, like whirlwind's rage,
Amidst a crew of thy confederates, 30
And clap me up where none might come at me,
Nor I at any to reveal my wrongs.
What madding fury did possess thy wits?
Or wherein is't that I offended thee?

LORENZO.
Advise you better, Bel-imperia, 35
For I have done you no disparagement;
Unless, by more discretion than deserv'd,
I sought to save your honor and mine own.

BEL-IMPERIA.
Mine honor! Why, Lorenzo, wherein is't
That I neglect my reputation so, 40
As you, or any, need to rescue it?

LORENZO.
His highness and my father were resolv'd
To come confer with old Hieronimo
Concerning certain matters of estate
That by the viceroy was determined. 45

BEL-IMPERIA.
And wherein was mine honor touch'd in that?

BALTHAZAR.
Have patience, Bel-imperia; hear the rest.

LORENZO.
Me, next in sight, as messenger they sent
To give him notice that they were so nigh.
Now, when I came, consorted with the prince, 50
And unexpected in an arbor there
Found Bel-imperia with Horatio—

BEL-IMPERIA.
How then?

---

28. *company*] companion.
36. *disparagement*] humiliation, disgrace.
45. *That . . . determined*] the possession of which was ended or given up.
46. *touch'd*] affected.

LORENZO.
    Why, then, rememb'ring that old disgrace,
    Which you for Don Andrea had endur'd,   55
    And now were likely longer to sustain,
    By being found so meanly accompanied,
    Thought rather, for I knew no readier mean,
    To thrust Horatio forth my father's way.
BALTHAZAR.
    And carry you obscurely somewhere else,   60
    Lest that his highness should have found you there.
BEL-IMPERIA.
    Even so, my lord? And you are witness
    That this is true which he entreateth of?
    You, gentle brother, forged this for my sake,
    And you, my lord, were made his instrument!   65
    A work of worth, worthy the noting too!
    But what's the cause that you conceal'd me since?
LORENZO.
    Your melancholy, sister, since the news
    Of your first favorite Don Andrea's death,
    My father's old wrath hath exasperate.   70
BALTHAZAR.
    And better was't for you, being in disgrace,
    To absent yourself, and give his fury place.
BEL-IMPERIA.
    But why had I no notice of his ire?
LORENZO.
    That were to add more fuel to your fire,
    Who burnt like Aetna for Andrea's loss.   75
BEL-IMPERIA.
    Hath not my father then inquir'd for me?
LORENZO.
    Sister, he hath; and thus excus'd I thee:
                        He whispereth in her ear.
    But Bel-imperia, see the gentle prince;
    Look on thy love, behold young Balthazar,
    Whose passions by thy presence are increas'd;   80

75. for] *Qq;* and *MSR.*

---

59. *forth*] out of.   70. *exasperate*] made more violent.

III.x   THE SPANISH TRAGEDY

    And in whose melancholy thou mayest see
    Thy hate, his love; thy flight, his following thee.
BEL-IMPERIA.
    Brother, you are become an orator—
    I know not, I, by what experience—
    Too politic for me, past all compare,   85
    Since last I saw you; but content yourself:
    The prince is meditating higher things.
BALTHAZAR.
    'Tis of thy beauty, then, that conquers kings;
    Of those thy tresses, Ariadne's twines,
    Wherewith my liberty thou hast surpris'd;   90
    Of that thine ivory front, my sorrow's map,
    Wherein I see no haven to rest my hope.
BEL-IMPERIA.
    To love and fear, and both at once, my lord,
    In my conceit, are things of more import
    Than women's wits are to be busied with.   95
BALTHAZAR.
    'Tis I that love.
BEL-IMPERIA.   Whom?
BALTHAZAR.   Bel-imperia.
BEL-IMPERIA.
    But I that fear.
BALTHAZAR.   Whom?
BEL-IMPERIA.   Bel-imperia.
LORENZO.
    Fear yourself?
BEL-IMPERIA.   Ay, brother.
LORENZO.   How?
BEL-IMPERIA.   As those
    That what they love are loth and feard to lose.

99. feard] *this edn.;* feare *Qq.*

---

    89. *Ariadne*] who used a thread (twine) to guide Theseus through the labyrinth. Confused with Arachne? (E).
    90. *surpris'd*] captured.
    91. *front*] forehead.
    91. *map*] picture of.
    94. *conceit*] conception, thinking.
    99. *feard*] afraid.

BALTHAZAR.
   Then, fair, let Balthazar your keeper be.   100
BEL-IMPERIA.
   No, Balthazar doth fear as well as we:
   Et tremulo metui pavidum junxere timorem—
   Est vanum stolidae proditionis opus.   *Exit.*
LORENZO.
   Nay, and you argue things so cunningly,
   We'll go continue this discourse at court.   105
BALTHAZAR.
   Led by the loadstar of her heavenly looks,
   Wends poor oppressed Balthazar,
   As o'er the mountains walks the wanderer,
   Incertain to effect his pilgrimage.   *Exeunt.*

[III.xi]   *Enter two* Portingales, *and* Hieronimo *meets them.*

1.
   By your leave, sir.

             [*Third passage of additions.*]
[HIERONIMO.
   'Tis neither as you think, nor as you think,
   Nor as you think; you're wide all:
   These slippers are not mine; they were my son Horatio's.
   My son—and what's a son? A thing begot   (5)
   Within a pair of minutes, thereabout;
   A lump bred up in darkness, and doth serve
   To ballace these light creatures we call women;
   And, at nine months' end, creeps forth to light.
   What is there yet in a son,   (10)

102. *Et*] *Hw; Est Qq.*   103. *Est*] *M, S; Et Qq.*

  102–103.] "And they joined fearful alarm to trembling fear—a vain work of senseless betrayal."
  104. *cunningly*] skilfully.
  109. *effect*] achieve, complete.
[III.xi]
  1. *By your leave*] excuse me.
  (*3*). *wide*] i.e., of the mark.
  (*8*). *ballace*] ballast.

III.xi   THE SPANISH TRAGEDY

To make a father dote, rave, or run mad?
Being born, it pouts, cries, and breeds teeth.
What is there yet in a son? He must be fed,
Be taught to go, and speak. Ay, or yet
Why might not a man love a calf as well?   (15)
Or melt in passion o'er a frisking kid,
As for a son? Methinks, a young bacon,
Or a fine little smooth horse-colt,
Should move a man as much as doth a son.
For one of these, in very little time,   (20)
Will grow to some good use; whereas a son,
The more he grows in stature and in years,
The more unsquar'd, unbevelled, he appears,
Reckons his parents among the rank of fools,
Strikes care upon their heads with his mad riots,   (25)
Makes them look old before they meet with age.
This is a son! And what a loss were this,
Considered truly? —Oh, but my Horatio
Grew out of reach of these insatiate humors;
He loved his loving parents;   (30)
He was my comfort, and his mother's joy,
The very arm that did hold up our house:
Our hopes were stored up in him.
None but a damned murderer could hate him.
He had not seen the back of nineteen year,   (35)
When his strong arm unhors'd
The proud prince Balthazar, and his great mind,
Too full of honor, took him unto mercy,
That valiant but ignoble Portingale.
Well, heaven is heaven still;   (40)
And there is Nemesis, and Furies,
And things called whips,

(*38*). him unto mercy] *B;* him vs   to mercy *Hz.*
to mercy *Qq, R;* to mercy *D;* him

(*14*). *go*] walk.
(*25*). *riots*] riotous behavior, excesses.
(*42*). *things called whips*] Cf. Armin, *Nest of Ninnies* (1608), p. 55: "Ther are, as Hamlet saies, things cald whips in store." Armin was probably thinking of *2 Henry VI*, II.i.137, "Have you not beadles in your town, and things called whips?"

—128—

And they sometimes do meet with murderers;
They do not always 'scape; that's some comfort.
Ay, ay, ay; and then time steals on, (*45*)
And steals, and steals, till violence leaps forth
Like thunder wrapp'd in a ball of fire,
And so doth bring confusion to them all.]

HIERONIMO.
Good leave have you; nay, I pray you go, 2 (*49*)
For I'll leave you, if you can leave me so.

2.
Pray you, which is the next way to my lord the duke's?

HIERONIMO.
The next way from me.

1.   To his house, we mean. 5 (*52*)

HIERONIMO.
Oh, hard by; 'tis yon house that you see.

2.
You could not tell us if his son were there?

HIERONIMO.
Who, my lord Lorenzo?

1.   Ay, sir.

He goeth in at one door and comes out at another.

HIERONIMO.   Oh, forbear!
For other talk for us far fitter were.
But if you be importunate to know 10 (*57*)
The way to him, and where to find him out,
Then list to me, and I'll resolve your doubt.
There is a path upon your left-hand side
That leadeth from a guilty conscience
Unto a forest of distrust and fear, 15 (*62*)
A darksome place, and dangerous to pass.
There shall you meet with melancholy thoughts,
Whose baleful humors if you but uphold,
It will conduct you to despair and death;
Whose rocky cliffs when you have once beheld, 20 (*67*)
Within a hugy dale of lasting night,
That, kindled with the world's iniquities,

13.] Cf. I.i.63; the path to "the deepest hell."
18. *humors*] melancholy was one of the four "humors," or vapors, in the human constitution.

III.xi THE SPANISH TRAGEDY

   Doth cast up filthy and detested fumes—
   Not far from thence, where murderers have built
   A habitation for their cursed souls,   25 *(72)*
   There, in a brazen caldron, fix'd by Jove,
   In his fell wrath, upon a sulphur flame,
   Yourselves shall find Lorenzo bathing him
   In boiling lead and blood of innocents.
1.
   Ha, ha, ha!
HIERONIMO. Ha, ha, ha!   30 *(77)*
   Why, ha, ha, ha! Farewell, good ha, ha, ha!   *Exit.*
2.
   Doubtless this man is passing lunatic,
   Or imperfection of his age doth make him dote.
   Come, let's away to seek my lord the duke.   *Exeunt.*

[III.xii]
  Enter Hieronimo, *with a poniard in one hand and a rope in the other.*

HIERONIMO.
   Now, sir, perhaps I come and see the king;
   The king sees me, and fain would hear my suit:
   Why, is not this a strange and seld-seen thing,
   That standers-by with toys should strike me mute?
   Go to; I see their shifts, and say no more.   5
   Hieronimo, 'tis time for thee to trudge:
   Down by the dale that flows with purple gore
   Standeth a fiery tower; there sits a judge
   Upon a seat of steel and molten brass,
   And 'twixt his teeth he holds a fire-brand,   10
   That leads unto the lake where hell doth stand.
   Away, Hieronimo! to him be gone:
   He'll do thee justice for Horatio's death.
   Turn down this path: thou shalt be with him straight;
   Or this, and then thou need'st not take thy breath: 15
   This way or that way? —Soft and fair, not so!
   For if I hang or kill myself, let's know

34.S.D.] *Q 4–10; not in Q 1–3.*

 3. *seld*] seldom.   4. *toys*] trifles.
 5. *shifts*] devices, tricks.   6. *trudge*] be gone.

THE SPANISH TRAGEDY   III.xii

Who will revenge Horatio's murder then?
No, no! fie, no! pardon me, I'll none of that.
He flings away the dagger and halter.
This way I'll take, and this way comes the king: 20
He takes them up again.
And here I'll have a fling at him; that's flat:
And, Balthazar, I'll be with thee to bring,
And thee, Lorenzo! Here's the king—nay, stay;
And here, ay here—there goes the hare away.

Enter King, Ambassador, Castile, *and* Lorenzo.

KING.
Now show, Ambassador, what our viceroy saith: 25
Hath he receiv'd the articles we sent?
HIERONIMO.
Justice, oh, justice to Hieronimo!
LORENZO.
Back! seest thou not the king is busy?
HIERONIMO.
Oh, is he so?
KING.
Who is he that interrupts our business?   30
HIERONIMO.
Not I. —Hieronimo, beware: go by, go by!
AMBASSADOR.
Renowned king, he hath received and read
Thy kingly proffers, and thy promis'd league;
And, as a man extremely overjoy'd
To hear his son so princely entertain'd,   35
Whose death he had so solemnly bewail'd,
This for thy further satisfaction
And kingly love he kindly lets thee know:
First, for the marriage of his princely son
With Bel-imperia, thy beloved niece,   40
The news are more delightful to his soul
Than myrrh or incense to the offended heavens.

---

22. *I'll ... bring*] I'll be even with you, bring you to reason, chastise you.
24. *there ... away*] Tilley, H 157; the quarry escapes.
31. *go by*] go aside, be careful.

−131−

III.xii   THE SPANISH TRAGEDY

  In person, therefore, will he come himself,
  To see the marriage rites solemnized,
  And, in the presence of the court of Spain,   45
  To knit a sure inexplicable band
  Of kingly love and everlasting league
  Betwixt the crowns of Spain and Portingale.
  There will he give his crown to Balthazar,
  And make a queen of Bel-imperia.   50
KING.
  Brother, how like you this our viceroy's love?
CASTILE.
  No doubt, my lord, it is an argument
  Of honorable care to keep his friend,
  And wondrous zeal to Balthazar his son;
  Nor am I least indebted to his grace,   55
  That bends his liking to my daughter thus.
AMBASSADOR.
  Now last, dread lord, here hath his highness sent
  (Although he send not that his son return)
  His ransom due to Don Horatio.
HIERONIMO.
  Horatio! Who calls Horatio?   60
KING.
  And well remember'd; thank his majesty.
  Here, see it given to Horatio.
HIERONIMO.
  Justice, oh, justice, justice, gentle king!
KING.
  Who is that? Hieronimo?
HIERONIMO.
  Justice, oh, justice! Oh, my son, my son,   65
  My son, whom naught can ransom or redeem!
LORENZO.
  Hieronimo, you are not well-advis'd.
HIERONIMO.
  Away, Lorenzo, hinder me no more;
  For thou hast made me bankrupt of my bliss.
  Give me my son! You shall not ransom him!   70

46. inexplicable] *Q2–10;* inexecrable *Q1;* inextricable *Hw.*

46. *inexplicable*] indissoluble.

Away! I'll rip the bowels of the earth,
He diggeth with his dagger.
And ferry over to th' Elysian plains,
And bring my son to show his deadly wounds.
Stand from about me!
I'll make a pickaxe of my poniard, 75
And here surrender up my marshalship:
For I'll go marshal up the fiends in hell,
To be avenged on you all for this.

KING.
What means this outrage?
Will none of you restrain his fury? 80

HIERONIMO.
Nay, soft and fair; you shall not need to strive:
Needs must he go that the devils drive. *Exit.*

KING.
What accident hath happ'd Hieronimo?
I have not seen him to demean him so.

LORENZO.
My gracious lord, he is with extreme pride, 85
Conceived of young Horatio, his son,
And covetous of having to himself
The ransom of the young prince Balthazar,
Distract, and in a manner lunatic.

KING.
Believe me, nephew, we are sorry for't; 90
This is the love that fathers bear their sons.—
But, gentle brother, go give to him this gold,
The prince's ransom; let him have his due,
For what he hath, Horatio shall not want;
Haply Hieronimo hath need thereof. 95

LORENZO.
But if he be thus helplessly distract,
'Tis requisite his office be resign'd,
And given to one of more discretion.

KING.
We shall increase his melancholy so.

95. Haply] *edd.;* Happily *Qq.*

82.] proverbial; Tilley, D 278.   83. *happ'd*] happened to.
84. *demean him*] behave.

III.xii   THE SPANISH TRAGEDY

> 'Tis best that we see further in it first,   100
> Till when, ourself will exempt the place.
> And, brother, now bring in the ambassador,
> That he may be a witness of the match
> 'Twixt Balthazar and Bel-imperia,
> And that we may prefix a certain time,   105
> Wherein the marriage shall be solemnized,
> That we may have thy lord, the viceroy, here.

AMBASSADOR.
> Therein your highness highly shall content
> His majesty, that longs to hear from hence.

KING.
> On, then, and hear you, Lord Ambassador—   *Exeunt.* 110

[*Fourth passage of additions.*]

[III.xiiA]   [*Enter* Jaques *and* Pedro.]

JAQUES.
> I wonder, Pedro, why our master thus
> At midnight sends us with our torches' light,
> When man and bird and beast are all at rest,
> Save those that watch for rape and bloody murder.

PEDRO.
> Oh Jaques, know thou that our master's mind   *(5)*
> Is much distraught, since his Horatio died,
> And—now his aged years should sleep in rest,
> His heart in quiet—like a desperate man,
> Grows lunatic and childish for his son.
> Sometimes, as he doth at his table sit,   *(10)*
> He speaks as if Horatio stood by him;
> Then starting in a rage, falls on the earth,
> Cries out, "Horatio! Where is my Horatio?"
> So that with extreme grief and cutting sorrow
> There is not left in him one inch of man.   *(15)*
> See, where he comes.

Enter Hieronimo.

---

    101. *exempt the place*] The Q sense is presumably "leave him in the post." The line is defective, and some emendation is probably required. "Keep immune from the necessity of replacing him" (O–S).
    105. *prefix*] fix in advance.

−134−

HIERONIMO.
    I pry through every crevice of each wall,
    Look on each tree, and search through every brake,
    Beat at the bushes, stamp our grandam earth,
    Dive in the water, and stare up to heaven,   (*20*)
    Yet cannot I behold my son Horatio.—
    How, now, who's there? sprites, sprites?
PEDRO.
    We are your servants that attend you, sir.
HIERONIMO.
    What make you with your torches in the dark?
PEDRO.
    You bid us light them, and attend you here.   (*25*)
HIERONIMO.
    No, no, you are deceiv'd!—not I; you are deceiv'd!
    Was I so mad to bid you light your torches now?
    Light me your torches at the mid of noon,
    Whenas the sun-god rides in all his glory;
    Light me your torches then.
PEDRO.   Then we burn daylight.   (*30*)
HIERONIMO.
    Let it be burnt; Night is a murderous slut,
    That would not have her treasons to be seen;
    And yonder pale-faced Hecate there, the moon,
    Doth give consent to that is done in darkness;
    And all those stars that gaze upon her face,   (*35*)
    Are aglets on her sleeve, pins on her train;
    And those that should be powerful and divine
    Do sleep in darkness when they most should shine.
PEDRO.
    Provoke them not, fair sir, with tempting words;
    The heavens are gracious, and your miseries   (*40*)
    And sorrow makes you speak you know not what.
HIERONIMO.
    Villain, thou liest! and thou doest naught
    But tell me I am mad: thou liest! I am not mad!

  (*18*). *brake*] thicket.
  (*30*). *burn daylight*] proverbial for waste of time; cf. Tilley, D 123; Shakespeare, *Romeo and Juliet*, I.iv.43; *Merry Wives of Windsor*, II.i.54.
  (*36*). *aglets*] metallic studs, plates or spangles worn on a dress.

III.xiiA   THE SPANISH TRAGEDY

    I know thee to be Pedro, and he Jaques.
    I'll prove it to thee; and were I mad, how could I?   (*45*)
    Where was she that same night when my Horatio
    Was murdered? She should have shone; search thou the book.
    Had the moon shone, in my boy's face there was a kind of grace,
    That I know—nay, I do know—had the murderer seen him,
    His weapon would have fall'n and cut the earth,   (*50*)
    Had he been framed of naught but blood and death.
    Alack, when mischief doth it knows not what,
    What shall we say to mischief?

                Enter Isabella.

ISABELLA.
    Dear Hieronimo, come in a' doors;
    Oh, seek not means so to increase thy sorrow.   (*55*)
HIERONIMO.
    Indeed, Isabella, we do nothing here;
    I do not cry—ask Pedro, and ask Jaques;
    Not I, indeed; we are merry, very merry.
ISABELLA.
    How? be merry here, be merry here?
    Is not this the place, and this the very tree,   (*60*)
    Where my Horatio died, where he was murdered?
HIERONIMO.
    Was—do not say what; let her weep it out.
    This was the tree; I set it of a kernel;
    And when our hot Spain could not let it grow,
    But that the infant and the human sap   (*65*)
    Began to wither, duly twice a morning
    Would I be sprinkling it with fountain water.
    At last it grew, and grew, and bore, and bore,
    Till at the length
    It grew a gallows and did bear our son;   (*70*)
    It bore thy fruit and mine—oh wicked plant!
                One knocks within at the door.
    See who knocks there.
PEDRO.   It is a painter, sir.

(*58*). are] *this edn.;* are very *Q4–10*.
(*61*). died] *Q5–10* (dyed); hied *Q4*.
(*71*). wicked] *Q5;* wicked, wicked *Q4, 6–10*.
(*72*). knocks] *Q5–10;* knocke *Q4*.

-136-

THE SPANISH TRAGEDY   III.xiiA

HIERONIMO.
    Bid him come in, and paint some comfort;
    For surely there's none lives but painted comfort.
    Let him come in! —One knows not what may chance: *(75)*
    God's will that I should set this tree! —But even so
    Masters ungrateful servants rear from naught,
    And then they hate them that did bring them up.

Enter the Painter.

PAINTER.
    God bless you, sir.
HIERONIMO.   Wherefore? Why, thou scornful villain?
    How, where, or by what means should I be bless'd?   *(80)*
ISABELLA.
    What wouldst thou have, good fellow?
PAINTER.   Justice, madam.
HIERONIMO.
    Oh ambitious beggar,
    Wouldst thou have that that lives not in the world?
    Why, all the undelved mines cannot buy
    An ounce of justice, 'tis a jewel so inestimable.   *(85)*
    I tell thee, God hath engrossed all justice in his hands,
    And there is none but what comes from him.
PAINTER.   Oh, then I see
    That God must right me for my murder'd son.
HIERONIMO.
    How, was thy son murdered?
PAINTER.
    Ay, sir; no man did hold a son so dear.   *(90)*
HIERONIMO.
    What, not as thine? That's a lie,
    As massy as the earth. I had a son
    Whose least unvalued hair did weigh
    A thousand of thy son's; and he was murdered.
PAINTER.
    Alas, sir, I had no more but he.   *(95)*
HIERONIMO.
    Nor I, nor I; but this same one of mine

(77). rear] *Q4* (reare); reard *Q5–10*.

III.xiiA   THE SPANISH TRAGEDY

  Was worth a legion. But all is one.
  Pedro, Jaques, go in a' doors; Isabella, go;
  And this good fellow here and I
  Will range this hideous orchard up and down,   (*100*)
  Like to two lions reaved of their young.
  Go in a' doors, I say.   *Exeunt. The* Painter *and he sits down.*
    Come, let's talk wisely now.
  Was thy son murdered?
PAINTER.   Ay, sir.
HIERONIMO.   So was mine.
  How dost take it? Art thou not sometimes mad?
  Is there no tricks that comes before thine eyes?   (*105*)
PAINTER.
  Oh Lord, yes, sir.
HIERONIMO.
  Art a painter? Canst paint me a tear, or a wound, a groan,
  or a sigh? Canst paint me such a tree as this?
PAINTER.
  Sir, I am sure you have heard of my painting; my name's
  Bazardo.   (*110*)
HIERONIMO.
  Bazardo! Afore God, an excellent fellow. Look you, sir, do
  you see? I'd have you paint me in my gallery, in your oil-
  colors matted, and draw me five years younger than I am—
  do ye see, sir, let five years go, let them go—like the Marshal
  of Spain; my wife Isabella standing by me, with a speaking (*115*)
  look to my son Horatio, which should intend to this or some
  such like purpose: "God bless thee, my sweet son"; and
  my hand leaning upon his head, thus, sir, do you see? May
  it be done?
PAINTER.
  Very well, sir.   (*120*)
HIERONIMO.
  Nay, I pray mark me, sir. Then sir, would I have you paint
  me this tree, this very tree. Canst paint a doleful cry?

(*102*). a' doors] *Q4, 6–10* (a   (*108*). tree] *Q4, 6–10;* teare *Q5.*
doores); at doores *Q5.*   (*112*). in my] *Lamb. E;* my *Qq.*

 (*101*). *reaved*] bereaved, reft.
 (*105*). *tricks*] illusions.

THE SPANISH TRAGEDY   III.xiiA

PAINTER.
    Seemingly, sir.
HIERONIMO.
    Nay, it should cry; but all is one. Well, sir, paint me a
    youth run thorough and thorough with villains' swords, *(125)*
    hanging upon this tree. Canst thou draw a murderer?
PAINTER.
    I'll warrant you, sir; I have the pattern of the most
    notorious villains that ever lived in all Spain.
HIERONIMO.
    Oh, let them be worse, worse; stretch thine art, and let
    their beards be of Judas his own color; and let their eye- *(130)*
    brows jutty over—in any case observe that. Then, sir, after
    some violent noise, bring me forth in my shirt, and my
    gown under mine arm, with my torch in my hand, and my
    sword reared up, thus—and with these words:
        "What noise is this? Who calls Hieronimo?"   *(135)*
    May it be done?
PAINTER.
    Yea, sir.
HIERONIMO.
    Well, sir; then bring me forth, bring me thorough alley and
    alley, still with a distracted countenance going along, and
    let my hair heave up my nightcap. Let the clouds scowl, *(140)*
    make the moon dark, the stars extinct, the winds blowing,
    the bells tolling, the owl shrieking, the toads croaking, the
    minutes jarring, and the clock striking twelve. And then at
    last, sir, starting, behold a man hanging, and tottering, and
    tottering, as you know the wind will wave a man, and I *(145)*
    with a trice to cut him down. And looking upon him by the
    advantage of my torch, find it to be my son Horatio. There
    you may show a passion, there you may show a passion!
    Draw me like old Priam of Troy, crying, "The house is
    afire, the house is afire, as the torch over my head!" *(150)*
    Make me curse, make me rave, make my cry, make me

(145). wave] *Q5;* weaue *Q4, 6–10.*   *(148)*. may show] *S, B;* may *Qq.*

---

(123). *Seemingly*] realistically.   *(130)*. *Judas . . . color*] red.
(131). *jutty*] jut, project.   *(138)*. *alley*] garden-walk.
(143). *jarring*] ticking.   *(145)*. *wave*] sway.
(146). *with a trice*] in a trice.   *(148)*. *passion*] fit of emotion.

III.xiiA　　　THE SPANISH TRAGEDY

mad, make me well again, make me curse hell, invocate heaven, and in the end leave me in a trance— and so forth.

PAINTER.
　　And is this the end? (155)
HIERONIMO.
　　Oh no, there is no end; the end is death and madness. As I am never better than when I am mad; then methinks I am a brave fellow; then I do wonders; but reason abuseth me, and there's the torment, there's the hell. At the last, sir, bring me to one of the murderers; were he as strong as (160) Hector, thus would I tear and drag him up and down.
　　He beats the Painter in, then comes out again, with a book in his hand.]

[III.xiii]　　*Enter Hieronimo, with a book in his hand.*

HIERONIMO.
　　Vindicta mihi!
　Ay, Heaven will be revenged of every ill;
　Nor will they suffer murder unrepaid.
　Then stay, Hieronimo, attend their will;
　For mortal men may not appoint their time. 5
　Per scelus semper tutum est sceleribus iter:
　Strike, and strike home, where wrong is offer'd thee;
　For evils unto ills conductors be,
　And death's the worst of resolution.
　For he that thinks with patience to contend 10
　To quiet life, his life shall easily end.—
　Fata si miseros juvant, habes salutem;
　Fata si vitam negant, habes sepulchrum:

0.1.] *Q1–3; replaced in Q4–10 by* 1. S.P. HIERONIMO] *edd.; not in Qq. III.xiiA final S.D.*

(*158*). *abuseth*] deceiveth.
[III.xiii]
　0.1. *a book*] Seneca; cf. l. 6 below.
　1. *Vindicta mihi!*] The biblical "Vengeance is mine; I will repay, saith the Lord" (Romans 12:19).
　6.] An adaptation of Seneca *Agamemnon* 115: *per scelera semper sceleribus est iter* (The safe path to crimes is always through crimes).
　9. *the worst of*] the worst that can follow from.
　10. *contend*] strive, persevere.
　12–13.] Seneca *Troades* 510–512, expounded and applied in the following lines.

THE SPANISH TRAGEDY   III.xiii

If destiny thy miseries do ease,
Then hast thou health, and happy shalt thou be.   15
If destiny deny thee life, Hieronimo,
Yet shalt thou be assured of a tomb;
If neither, yet let this thy comfort be:
Heaven covereth him that hath no burial.
And to conclude, I will revenge his death.   20
But how? Not as the vulgar wits of men,
With open, but inevitable ills,
As by a secret, yet a certain mean,
Which under kindship will be cloaked best.
Wise men will take their opportunity,   25
Closely and safely fitting things to time.
But in extremes advantage hath no time;
And therefore all times fit not for revenge.
Thus therefore will I rest me in unrest,
Dissembling quiet in unquietness,   30
Not seeming that I know their villainies,
That my simplicity may make them think
That ignorantly I will let all slip;
For ignorance, I wot, and well they know,
Remedium malorum iners est.   35
Nor aught avails it me to menace them,
Who, as a wintry storm upon a plain,
Will bear me down with their nobility.
No, no, Hieronimo, thou must enjoin
Thine eyes to observation, and thy tongue   40
To milder speeches than thy spirit affords,
Thy heart to patience, and thy hands to rest,
Thy cap to courtesy, and thy knee to bow,
Till to revenge thou know when, where, and how.
                                  A noise within.

44.1.] *Q 4–10; after l. 45 in Q 1–3.*

19.] Lucan *Pharsalia* vii. 118: *Caelo tegitur qui non habet urnam* (S).
21. *vulgar wits*] common or ordinary intelligences.
23. *As*] for example.
24. *kindship*] kindness.
27.] In desperate situations one cannot await a favorable opportunity.
32. *simplicity*] apparent naïveté, ingenuousness.
35.] Seneca *Oedipus* 515: *Iners malorum remedium ignorantia est* (Ignorance is an idle remedy for ills).

III.xiii   The Spanish Tragedy

       How now, what noise? What coil is that you keep?   45

              Enter a Servant.

SERVANT.
       Here are a sort of poor petitioners
       That are importunate, and it shall please you, sir.
       That you should plead their cases to the king.
HIERONIMO.
       That I should plead their several actions?
       Why, let them enter, and let me see them.   50

            Enter three Citizens *and an* Old Man.

1.
       So; I tell you this: for learning and for law,
       There is not any advocate in Spain
       That can prevail, or will take half the pain
       That he will, in pursuit of equity.
HIERONIMO.
       Come near, you men, that thus importune me.—   55
       Now must I bear a face of gravity;
       For thus I us'd, before my marshalship,
       To plead in causes as corregidor.—
       Come on, sirs, what's the matter?
2.   Sir, an action.
HIERONIMO.
       Of battery?
1.   Mine of debt.
HIERONIMO.   Give place.   60
2.
       No, sir, mine is an action of the case.
3.
       Mine an *ejectione firmae* by a lease.

62. *firmae*] *S*; *firma Qq*.

---

    45. *coil . . . keep*] disturbance . . . make.
    46. *sort*] group.
    47. *and*] if.
    49. *actions*] cases, petitions.
    58. *corregidor*] properly, magistrate; here, advocate.
    61. *action . . . case*] a plea in which the whole case was set out in the original writ, not being covered by the normal jurisdiction of the court.
    62. *ejectione firmae*] a writ to eject a tenant before his lease expires.

THE SPANISH TRAGEDY   III.xiii

HIERONIMO.
    Content you, sirs; are you determined
    That I should plead your several actions?
1.
    Ay, sir, and here's my declaration.   65
2.
    And here is my band.
3.   And here is my lease.   *They give him papers.*
HIERONIMO.
    But wherefore stands yon silly man so mute,
    With mournful eyes and hands to heaven uprear'd?
    Come hither, father, let me know thy cause.
SENEX.
    Oh worthy sir, my cause, but slightly known,   70
    May move the hearts of warlike Myrmidons,
    And melt the Corsic rocks with ruthful tears.
HIERONIMO.
    Say, father, tell me, what's thy suit?
SENEX.
    No, sir; could my woes
    Give way unto my most distressful words,   75
    Then should I not in paper, as you see,
    With ink bewray what blood began in me.
HIERONIMO.
    What's here? "The humble supplication
    Of Don Bazulto for his murder'd son."
SENEX.
    Ay sir.
HIERONIMO.   No, sir; it was my murder'd son!   80
    Oh my son, my son, oh my son Horatio!
    But mine, or thine, Bazulto, be content.
    Here, take my handkercher and wipe thine eyes,
    Whiles wretched I in thy mishaps may see
    The lively portrait of my dying self.   85
          He draweth out a bloody napkin.

---

66. *band*] bond.
67. *silly*] simple, poor.
69. *father*] old man.
71. *Myrmidons*] the soldiers of Achilles at Troy.
72. *Corsic rocks*] Seneca *Octavia* 382, "Corsica rupes" (S).

III.xiii THE SPANISH TRAGEDY

   Oh no, not this; Horatio, this was thine;
   And when I dy'd it in thy dearest blood,
   This was a token 'twixt thy soul and me
   That of thy death revenged I should be.
   But here, take this, and this—what, my purse?—   90
   Ay, this, and that, and all of them are thine;
   For all as one are our extremities.
1.
   Oh, see the kindness of Hieronimo!
2.
   This gentleness shows him a gentleman.
HIERONIMO.
   See, see, oh, see thy shame, Hieronimo!   95
   See here a loving father to his son!
   Behold the sorrows and the sad laments,
   That he delivereth for his son's decease!
   If love's effects so strives in lesser things,
   If love enforce such moods in meaner wits,   100
   If love express such power in poor estates:
   Hieronimo, when as a raging sea,
   Toss'd with the wind and tide, o'erturneth then
   The upper billows, course of waves to keep,
   Whilst lesser waters labor in the deep,   105
   Then shamest thou not, Hieronimo, to neglect
   The sweet revenge of thy Horatio?
   Though on this earth justice will not be found,
   I'll down to hell, and in this passion
   Knock at the dismal gates of Pluto's court,   110
   Getting by force, as once Alcides did,
   A troop of Furies and tormenting hags
   To torture Don Lorenzo and the rest.
   Yet, lest the triple-headed porter should
   Deny my passage to the slimy strond,   115
   The Thracian poet thou shalt counterfeit.
   Come on, old father, be my Orpheus,
   And if thou canst no notes upon the harp,

103. o'erturneth] *Hw;* oreturnest
Q1–7; ore-turned *Q8–10.*

 111. *Alcides*] Hercules.   114. *porter*] Cerberus.
 118. *canst*] knowest.

The Spanish Tragedy   III.xiii

    Then sound the burden of thy sore heart's grief,
    Till we do gain that Proserpine may grant   120
    Revenge on them that murdered my son.
    Then will I rent and tear them, thus, and thus,
    Shivering their limbs in pieces with my teeth.   *Tear the papers.*

1.
    Oh sir, my declaration!   *Exit* Hieronimo, *and they after.*
2.
    Save my bond!   125

        Enter Hieronimo.
2.
    Save my bond!
3.
    Alas, my lease! it cost me ten pound, and you, my lord, have
    torn the same.

HIERONIMO.
    That cannot be; I gave it never a wound;
    Show me one drop of blood fall from the same!   130
    How is it possible I should slay it, then?
    Tush, no; run after, catch me if you can.

Exeunt all but the Old Man. Bazulto *remains till* Hieronimo *enters again, who, staring him in the face, speaks.*

HIERONIMO.
    And art thou come, Horatio, from the depth,
    To ask for justice in this upper earth,
    To tell thy father thou art unreveng'd,   135
    To wring more tears from Isabella's eyes,
    Whose lights are dimm'd with over-long laments?
    Go back, my son; complain to Aeacus,
    For here's no justice; gentle boy, begone,
    For justice is exiled from the earth;   140
    Hieronimo will bear thee company.
    Thy mother cries on righteous Rhadamanth
    For just revenge against the murderers.

SENEX.
    Alas, my lord, whence springs this troubled speech?

---

  119. *burden*] (*a*) refrain; (*b*) heavy load.
  138, 142. *Aeacus, Rhadamanth*] see I.i.33 n.

III.xiii   THE SPANISH TRAGEDY

HIERONIMO.
> But let me look on my Horatio.   145
> Sweet boy, how art thou chang'd in death's black shade!
> Had Proserpine no pity on thy youth,
> But suffered thy fair crimson-color'd spring
> With withered winter to be blasted thus?
> Horatio, thou art older than thy father: 150
> Ah, ruthless fate, that favor thus transforms!

BAZULTO.
> Ah, my good lord, I am not your young son.

HIERONIMO.
> What, not my son? Thou then a Fury art,
> Sent from the empty kingdom of black night
> To summon me to make appearance   155
> Before grim Minos and just Rhadamanth,
> To plague Hieronimo that is remiss,
> And seeks not vengeance for Horatio's death.

BAZULTO.
> I am a grieved man, and not a ghost,
> That came for justice for my murdered son.   160

HIERONIMO.
> Ay, now I know thee, now thou namest thy son:
> Thou art the lively image of my grief;
> Within thy face my sorrows I may see.
> Thy eyes are gumm'd with tears, thy cheeks are wan,
> Thy forehead troubled, and thy mutt'ring lips   165
> Murmur sad words abruptly broken off,
> By force of windy sighs thy spirit breathes;
> And all this sorrow riseth for thy son,
> And selfsame sorrow feel I for my son.
> Come in, old man, thou shalt to Isabel.   170
> Lean on my arm; I thee, thou me shalt stay;
> And thou, and I, and she, will sing a song,
> Three parts in one, but all of discords fram'd.—
> Talk not of cords, but let us now be gone;
> For with a cord Horatio was slain.   *Exeunt.* 175

151. fate] *D;* Father *Qq.*   161. thy] *Q9–10;* my *Q1–8.*

---

151. *favor*] the face, countenance.
171. *stay*] support.

[III.xiv]
Enter [on one side] King of Spain, *the* Duke, Lorenzo, Balthazar, Bel-imperia, [*and Attendants; and, on the other,*] Viceroy, Don Pedro, [*and Attendants*].

KING.
  Go, brother, it is the Duke of Castile's cause;
  Salute the viceroy in our name.
CASTILE.   I go.
VICEROY.
  Go forth, Don Pedro, for thy nephew's sake,
  And greet the Duke of Castile.
PEDRO.   It shall be so.
KING.
  And now to meet these Portuguese;   5
  For, as we now are, so sometimes were these,
  Kings and commanders of the western Indies.
  Welcome, brave viceroy, to the court of Spain,
  And welcome all his honorable train!
  'Tis not unknown to us for why you come,   10
  Or have so kingly cross'd the seas.
  Sufficeth it, in this we note the troth
  And more than common love you lend to us.
  So is it that mine honorable niece
  (For it beseems us now that it be known)   15
  Already is betroth'd to Balthazar;
  And by appointment and our condescent
  Tomorrow are they to be married.
  To this intent we entertain thyself,
  Thy followers, their pleasure, and our peace.   20
  Speak, men of Portingale, shall it be so?
  If ay, say so; if not, say flatly no.
VICEROY.
  Renowned king, I come not, as thou think'st,
  With doubtful followers, unresolved men,

0.1–3] *Qq* (Enter King of Spain, Balthazar, Don Pedro, *and* Bel-*the* Duke, Vice-roy, *and* Lorenzo, imperia.)

6–7.] inaccurate, especially as to "sometimes" (formerly). The Portuguese did have the *East* Indies.
17. *condescent*] consent.

But such as have upon thine articles 25
Confirmed thy motion, and contented me.
Know, sovereign, I come to solemnize
The marriage of thy beloved niece,
Fair Bel-imperia, with my Balthazar—
With thee, my son; whom sith I live to see, 30
Here take my crown; I give it her and thee;
And let me live a solitary life,
In ceaseless prayers,
To think how strangely heaven hath thee preserved.

KING.
See, brother, see, how nature strives in him! 35
Come, worthy viceroy, and accompany
Thy friend with thine extremities;
A place more private fits this princely mood.

VICEROY.
Or here, or where your highness thinks it good.

Exeunt all but Castile *and* Lorenzo.

CASTILE.
Nay, stay, Lorenzo; let me talk with you. 40
Seest thou this entertainment of these kings?

LORENZO.
I do, my lord, and joy to see the same.

CASTILE.
And knowest thou why this meeting is?

LORENZO.
For her, my lord, whom Balthazar doth love,
And to confirm their promised marriage. 45

CASTILE.
She is thy sister?

LORENZO. Who, Bel-imperia? Ay,
My gracious lord, and this is the day
That I have long'd so happily to see.

CASTILE.
Thou wouldst be loth that any fault of thine
Should intercept her in her happiness? 50

---

37. *extremities*] extremes of emotion.
50. *intercept*] obstruct, hinder.

LORENZO.
    Heavens will not let Lorenzo err so much.
CASTILE.
    Why then, Lorenzo, listen to my words:
    It is suspected, and reported too,
    That thou, Lorenzo, wrong'st Hieronimo,
    And in his suits towards his majesty   55
    Still keep'st him back, and seeks to cross his suit.
LORENZO.
    That I, my lord—?
CASTILE.
    I tell thee, son, myself have heard it said,
    When, to my sorrow, I have been ashamed
    To answer for thee, though thou art my son.   60
    Lorenzo, knowest thou not the common love
    And kindness that Hieronimo hath won
    By his deserts within the court of Spain?
    Or seest thou not the king my brother's care
    In his behalf, and to procure his health?   65
    Lorenzo, shouldst thou thwart his passions,
    And he exclaim against thee to the king,
    What honor were't in this assembly,
    Or what a scandal were't among the kings
    To hear Hieronimo exclaim on thee?   70
    Tell me—and look thou tell me truly too—
    Whence grows the ground of this report in court?
LORENZO.
    My lord, it lies not in Lorenzo's power
    To stop the vulgar, liberal of their tongues:
    A small advantage makes a water-breach,   75
    And no man lives that long contenteth all.
CASTILE.
    Myself have seen thee busy to keep back
    Him and his supplications from the king.
LORENZO.
    Yourself, my lord, hath seen his passions,

---

  51. *err*] go astray.
  74. *liberal*] too free, licentious.
   75. *advantage*] opportunity, i.e., a small breach, which becomes a large one.

III.xiv   THE SPANISH TRAGEDY

    That ill beseem'd the presence of a king;   80
    And for I pitied him in his distress,
    I held him thence with kind and courteous words
    As free from malice to Hieronimo
    As to my soul, my lord.
CASTILE.
    Hieronimo, my son, mistakes thee then.   85
LORENZO.
    My gracious father, believe me, so he doth.
    But what's a silly man, distract in mind
    To think upon the murder of his son?
    Alas, how easy is it for him to err!
    But for his satisfaction and the world's,   90
    'Twere good, my lord, that Hieronimo and I
    Were reconcil'd, if he misconster me.
CASTILE.
    Lorenzo, thou hast said; it shall be so.—
    Go one of you, and call Hieronimo.

            Enter Balthazar *and* Bel-imperia.

BALTHAZAR.
    Come, Bel-imperia, Balthazar's content,   95
    My sorrow's ease and sovereign of my bliss,
    Sith heaven hath ordain'd thee to be mine;
    Disperse those clouds and melancholy looks,
    And clear them up with those thy sun-bright eyes,
    Wherein my hope and heaven's fair beauty lies.   100
BEL-IMPERIA.
    My looks, my lord, are fitting for my love,
    Which, new-begun, can show no brighter yet.
BALTHAZAR.
    New-kindled flames should burn as morning sun.
BEL-IMPERIA.
    But not too fast, lest heat and all be done.
    I see my lord my father.
BALTHAZAR.   Truce, my love;   105
    I will go salute him.

102. no] *Q 2–10; not in Q 1.*

  81. *for*] because.
  92. *misconster*] misconstrue.

THE SPANISH TRAGEDY   III.xiv

CASTILE.   Welcome, Balthazar,
   Welcome, brave prince, the pledge of Castile's peace;
   And welcome, Bel-imperia. —How now, girl?
   Why comest thou sadly to salute us thus?
   Content thyself, for I am satisfied.   110
   It is not now as when Andrea liv'd;
   We have forgotten and forgiven that,
   And thou art graced with a happier love.—
   But, Balthazar, here comes Hieronimo;
   I'll have a word with him.   115

              Enter Hieronimo *and a* Servant.

HIERONIMO.
   And where's the duke?
SERVANT.   Yonder.
HIERONIMO.   Even so.—
   What new device have they devised, trow?
   Pocas palabras! mild as the lamb!
   Is't I will be reveng'd? No, I am not the man.
CASTILE.
   Welcome, Hieronimo.   120
LORENZO.
   Welcome, Hieronimo.
BALTHAZAR.
   Welcome, Hieronimo.
HIERONIMO.
   My lords, I thank you for Horatio.
CASTILE.
   Hieronimo, the reason that I sent
   To speak with you, is this.
HIERONIMO.   What, so short?   125
   Then I'll be gone; I thank you для't.
CASTILE.
   Nay, stay, Hieronimo! —Go, call him, son.
LORENZO.
   Hieronimo, my father craves a word with you.
HIERONIMO.
   With me, sir? —Why, my lord, I thought you had done.

128. S.P. LORENZO] *Q2–10; not in Q1.*

   117. *trow?*] think you?   118. *Pocas palabras*] few words.

                              −151−

III.xiv   THE SPANISH TRAGEDY

LORENZO.
    No. —[*Aside.*] Would he had!
CASTILE.   Hieronimo, I hear   130
    You find yourself aggrieved at my son,
    Because you have not access unto the king;
    And say 'tis he that intercepts your suits.
HIERONIMO.
    Why, is not this a miserable thing, my lord?
CASTILE.
    Hieronimo, I hope you have no cause,   135
    And would be loth that one of your deserts
    Should once have reason to suspect my son,
    Considering how I think of you myself.
HIERONIMO.
    Your son Lorenzo! Whom, my noble lord?
    The hope of Spain, mine honorable friend?   140
    Grant me the combat of them, if they dare!
                                       Draws out his sword.
    I'll meet him face to face, to tell me so!
    These be the scandalous reports of such
    As love not me, and hate my lord too much.
    Should I suspect Lorenzo would prevent   145
    Or cross my suit, that loved my son so well?
    My lord, I am ashamed it should be said.
LORENZO.
    Hieronimo, I never gave you cause.
HIERONIMO.
    My good lord, I know you did not.
CASTILE.   There then pause;
    And for the satisfaction of the world,   150
    Hieronimo, frequent my homely house,
    The Duke of Castile, Cyprian's ancient seat;
    And when thou wilt, use me, my son, and it;
    But here, before prince Balthazar and me,
    Embrace each other, and be perfect friends.   155
HIERONIMO.
    Ay, marry, my lord, and shall.

144. love] *Q 6–10;* loues *Q 1–5.*

---

145. *prevent*] anticipate, forestall.
151. *homely*] hospitable.

–152–

THE SPANISH TRAGEDY   III.xv

Friends, quoth he? See, I'll be friends with you all!
Especially with you, my lovely lord;
For divers causes it is fit for us
That we be friends: the world is suspicious,   160
And men may think what we imagine not.
BALTHAZAR.
Why, this is friendly done, Hieronimo.
LORENZO.
And that, I hope, old grudges are forgot.
HIERONIMO.
What else? It were a shame it should not be so.
CASTILE.
Come on, Hieronimo, at my request;   165
Let us entreat your company today.
                    Exeunt [all but Hieronimo].
HIERONIMO.
Your lordship's to command. —Pha! keep your way:
Chi me fa più carezze che non suole,
Tradito mi ha, o tradir mi vuole.   *Exit.*

[III.xv]   [CHORUS]

GHOST.
Awake, Erichtho! Cerberus, awake!
Solicit Pluto, gentle Proserpine!
To combat, Acheron and Erebus!
For ne'er, by Styx and Phlegethon in hell,
O'er-ferried Charon to the fiery lakes   5
Such fearful sights as poor Andrea sees.
Revenge, awake!

158. Especially] *S*; Specially *Qq*. 1. Erichtho] *Qq* (*Erictha*); Alecto
159. fit] *Q 2–10*; sit *Q 1*.   *Hz.*
168–169.] *edd.; Mi. Chi mi fa?*   3. Erebus] *Hw*; Ericus *Qq*.
Pui Correzza Che non sule/ Tradito viha 3–5.] *S*; To combate *Achinon* and
otrade vule Q 1; later *Qq* more corrupt. *Ericus* in hell./ For neere by *Stix*
[III.xv]   and *Phlegeton*;/ Nor ferried *Caron* to
0.1.] Enter *Ghoast Qq.*   the fierie lakes *Qq*.

168–169.] "He who shows me more than customary affection has
betrayed me, or wishes to betray me."
[III.xv]
  1. *Erichtho*] a Thessalian sorceress.

–153–

III.xv   The Spanish Tragedy

REVENGE.
    Awake? For why?
GHOST.
    Awake, Revenge! for thou art ill-advis'd
    To sleep away what thou art warn'd to watch.   10
REVENGE.
    Content thyself, and do not trouble me.
GHOST.
    Awake, Revenge! if love—as love hath had—
    Have yet the power or prevalence in hell!
    Hieronimo with Lorenzo is join'd in league,
    And intercepts our passage to revenge.   15
    Awake, Revenge, or we are woebegone!
REVENGE.
    Thus worldings ground, what they have dream'd, upon.
    Content thyself, Andrea; though I sleep,
    Yet is my mood soliciting their souls.
    Sufficeth thee that poor Hieronimo   20
    Cannot forget his son Horatio.
    Nor dies Revenge, although he sleep awhile;
    For in unquiet, quietness is feign'd,
    And slumb'ring is a common worldly wile.
    Behold, Andrea, for an instance, how   25
    Revenge hath slept, and then imagine thou,
    What 'tis to be subject to destiny.

Enter a Dumb Show.

GHOST.
    Awake, Revenge; reveal this mystery.
REVENGE.
    The two first the nuptial torches bore
    As brightly burning as the midday's sun;   30
    But after them doth Hymen hie as fast,
    Clothed in sable and a saffron robe,

10.] *B;* Thsleepe, away, what, thou art warnd to watch *Q1;* with variations *Q2–9;* To sleep—awake; what thou art warn'd to watch! *Q10.*

    10. *what*] the time.
    17. *ground . . . upon*] found upon . . .; base their ideas on (their dreams).

—154—

And blows them out, and quencheth them with blood,
As discontent that things continue so.
GHOST.
Sufficeth me; thy meaning's understood, 35
And thanks to thee and those infernal powers
That will not tolerate a lover's woe.
Rest thee, for I will sit to see the rest.
REVENGE.
Then argue not, for thou hast thy request.
Exeunt [*Dumb Show*].

[IV.i]   *Enter* Bel-imperia *and* Hieronimo.
BEL-IMPERIA.
Is this the love thou bear'st Horatio?
Is this the kindness that thou counterfeits?
Are these the fruits of thine incessant tears?
Hieronimo, are these thy passions,
Thy protestations and thy deep laments, 5
That thou wert wont to weary men withal?
Oh unkind father! Oh deceitful world!
With what excuses canst thou show thyself
From this dishonor and the hate of men,
Thus to neglect the loss and life of him 10
Whom both my letters and thine own belief
Assures thee to be causeless slaughtered?
Hieronimo, for shame, Hieronimo,
Be not a history to aftertimes
Of such ingratitude unto thy son: 15
Unhappy mothers of such children then,
But monstrous fathers to forget so soon
The death of those whom they with care and cost
Have tender'd so, thus careless should be lost!
Myself, a stranger in respect of thee, 20
So loved his life, as still I wish their deaths.
Nor shall his death be unreveng'd by me,

9.] *most edd.;* With what dishonor   men? *Qq.*
and the hate of men,/ From this . . .

---

7. *unkind*] unnatural.   19. *tender'd*] cherished.
20. *in respect of*] compared to.

−155−

IV.i THE SPANISH TRAGEDY

  Although I bear it out for fashion's sake:
  For here I swear, in sight of heaven and earth,
  Shouldst thou neglect the love thou shouldst retain,   25
  And give it over and devise no more,
  Myself should send their hateful souls to hell
  That wrought his downfall with extremest death.
HIERONIMO.
  But may it be that Bel-imperia
  Vows such revenge as she hath deign'd to say?   30
  Why, then I see that heaven applies our drift,
  And all the saints do sit soliciting
  For vengeance on those cursed murderers.
  Madam, 'tis true, and now I find it so,
  I found a letter, written in your name,   35
  And in that letter, how Horatio died.
  Pardon, oh pardon, Bel-imperia,
  My fear and care in not believing it;
  Nor think I thoughtless think upon a mean
  To let his death be unreveng'd at full.   40
  And here I vow—so you but give consent,
  And will conceal my resolution—
  I will ere long determine of their deaths
  That causeless thus have murdered my son.
BEL-IMPERIA.
  Hieronimo, I will consent, conceal,   45
  And aught that may effect for thine avail
  Join with thee to revenge Horatio's death.
HIERONIMO.
  On, then; whatsoever I devise,
  Let me entreat you, grace my practices;
  For why the plot's already in mine head.   50
  Here they are.

31. applies] *Qq;* applauds *conj. C.*   44. murdered] *Q 4–10;* murderd *Q 1–3.*

---

 23. *bear it out*] pretend to accept it.
 31. *applies our drift*] supports our intention; is working in the same direction as we.
 38. *care*] caution.
 49. *grace my practices*] favor my schemes.
 50. *For why*] because.

THE SPANISH TRAGEDY   IV.i

Enter Balthazar *and* Lorenzo.

BALTHAZAR. How now, Hieronimo?
    What, courting Bel-imperia?
HIERONIMO. Ay, my lord;
    Such courting as, I promise you,
    She hath my heart; but you, my lord, have hers.
LORENZO.
    But now, Hieronimo, or never, we   55
    Are to entreat your help.
HIERONIMO. My help?
    Why, my good lords, assure yourselves of me;
    For you have given me cause—ay, by my faith have you!
BALTHAZAR.
    It pleas'd you, at the entertainment of the ambassador,
    To grace the king so much as with a show.   60
    Now, were your study so well furnished,
    As, for the passing of the first night's sport,
    To entertain my father with the like,
    Or any such like pleasing motion,
    Assure yourself, it would content them well.   65
HIERONIMO.
    Is this all?
BALTHAZAR.
    Ay, this is all.
HIERONIMO.
    Why then, I'll fit you; say no more.
    When I was young, I gave my mind
    And plied myself to fruitless poetry;   70
    Which though it profit the professor naught,
    Yet is it passing pleasing to the world.
LORENZO.
    And how for that?
HIERONIMO. Marry, my good lord, thus:—

---

54. *heart*] (*a*) affection; (*b*) secret.
60. *grace*] honor.
64. *motion*] show.
68. *fit*] (*a*) suit, provide; (*b*) deal with.
71. *professor*] practitioner.
72. *passing*] surpassingly, extremely.

IV.i   The Spanish Tragedy

    And yet methinks, you are too quick with us—
    When in Toledo there I studied,   75
    It was my chance to write a tragedy—
    See here, my lords—   *He shows them a book.*
    Which, long forgot, I found this other day.
    Now would your lordships favor me so much
    As but to grace me with your acting it—   80
    I mean, each one of you to play a part—
    Assure you it will prove most passing strange,
    And wondrous plausible to that assembly.
BALTHAZAR.
    What! would you have us play a tragedy?
HIERONIMO.
    Why, Nero thought it no disparagement,   85
    And kings and emperors have ta'en delight
    To make experience of their wits in plays.
LORENZO.
    Nay, be not angry, good Hieronimo;
    The prince but ask'd a question.
BALTHAZAR.
    In faith, Hieronimo, and you be in earnest,   90
    I'll make one.
LORENZO.
    And I another.
HIERONIMO.
    Now, my good lord, could you entreat
    Your sister, Bel-imperia, to make one?
    For what's a play without a woman in it?   95
BEL-IMPERIA.
    Little entreaty shall serve me, Hieronimo;
    For I must needs be employed in your play.
HIERONIMO.
    Why, this is well. I tell you, lordings,
    It was determined to have been acted
    By gentlemen and scholars too,   100
    Such as could tell what to speak.
BALTHAZAR.   And now
    It shall be play'd by princes and courtiers,

---

  83. *plausible*] likely to be applauded, pleasing.
  87. *experience*] trial.

Such as can tell how to speak—
If, as it is our country manner,
You will but let us know the argument.   105
HIERONIMO.
That shall I roundly. The chronicles of Spain
Record this written of a knight of Rhodes:
He was betrothed, and wedded at the length,
To one Perseda, an Italian dame,
Whose beauty ravished all that her beheld,   110
Especially the soul of Soliman,
Who at the marriage was the chiefest guest.
By sundry means sought Soliman to win
Perseda's love, and could not gain the same.
Then 'gan he break his passions to a friend,   115
One of his bashaws, whom he held full dear;
Her had this bashaw long solicited,
And saw she was not otherwise to be won
But by her husband's death, this knight of Rhodes,
Whom presently by treachery he slew.   120
She, stirr'd with an exceeding hate therefore,
As cause of this, slew Soliman,
And, to escape the bashaw's tyranny,
Did stab herself; and this the tragedy.
LORENZO.
Oh, excellent!
BEL-IMPERIA.   But say, Hieronimo,   125
What then became of him that was the bashaw?
HIERONIMO.
Marry, thus: moved with remorse of his misdeeds,
Ran to a mountain top, and hung himself.
BALTHAZAR.
But which of us is to perform that part?
HIERONIMO.
Oh, that will I, my lords; make no doubt of it: 130
I'll play the murderer, I warrant you;
For I already have conceited that.

---

104. *our country manner*] the manner of our country.
106. *roundly*] directly or thoroughly.
115. *break*] open, divulge.
116. *bashaws*] pashas.
132. *conceited*] conceived the idea of.

BALTHAZAR.
    And what shall I?
HIERONIMO.
    Great Soliman, the Turkish emperor.
LORENZO.
    And I?
HIERONIMO. Erastus, the knight of Rhodes.   135
BEL-IMPERIA.
    And I?
HIERONIMO. Perseda, chaste and resolute.
    And here, my lords, are several abstracts drawn,
    For each of you to note your parts,
    And act it, as occasion's offer'd you.
    You must provide a Turkish cap,   140
    A black mustachio, and a fauchion;
                  Gives a paper to **Balthazar.**
    You, with a cross, like to a knight of Rhodes;
                   Gives another to **Lorenzo.**
    And, madam, you must attire yourself
                   He giveth Bel-imperia *another.*
    Like Phoebe, Flora, or the Huntress,
    Which to your discretion shall seem best.   145
    And as for me, my lords, I'll look to one,
    And, with the ransom that the viceroy sent,
    So furnish and perform this tragedy
    As all the world shall say, Hieronimo
    Was liberal in gracing of it so.   150
BALTHAZAR.
    Hieronimo, methinks a comedy were better.
HIERONIMO.
    A comedy?
    Fie! comedies are fit for common wits;
    But to present a kingly troop withal,
    Give me a stately-written tragedy;   155
    Tragedia cothurnata, fitting kings,

---

    141. *fauchion*] falchion, a broad curved sword.
    144. *Huntress*] Diana.
    154. *troop*] company of actors.
    156. *Tragedia cothurnata*] buskined tragedy, i.e., high and stately.

Containing matter, and not common things.
My lords, all this must be performed,
As fitting for the first night's revelling.
The Italian tragedians were so sharp of wit,   160
That in one hour's meditation
They would perform anything in action.

LORENZO.
And well it may; for I have seen the like
In Paris 'mongst the French tragedians.

HIERONIMO.
In Paris? mass, and well remembered!   165
There's one thing more that rests for us to do.

BALTHAZAR.
What's that, Hieronimo? Forget not anything.

HIERONIMO.
Each one of us
Must act his part in unknown languages,
That it may breed the more variety: 170
As you, my lord, in Latin, I in Greek,
You in Italian; and, for because I know
That Bel-imperia hath practiced the French,
In courtly French shall all her phrases be.

BEL-IMPERIA.
You mean to try my cunning then, Hieronimo?   175

BALTHAZAR.
But this will be a mere confusion
And hardly shall we all be understood.

HIERONIMO.
It must be so; for the conclusion
Shall prove the invention and all was good.
And I myself in an oration,   180
And with a strange and wondrous show besides,
That I will have there behind a curtain,
Assure yourself, shall make the matter known;

---

179. invention] *edd.;* intention *Qq.*   181–182.] *Q 4–10, edd.; lines transposed in Q 1–3.*

160–162.] the extempore acting of the *commedia dell'arte.*
163. *may*] may be so.
179. *invention*] plot, subject matter.

IV.i   THE SPANISH TRAGEDY

   And all shall be concluded in one scene,
   For there's no pleasure ta'en in tediousness.   185
BALTHAZAR.
   How like you this?
LORENZO.   Why, thus, my lord,
   We must resolve to soothe his humors up.
BALTHAZAR.
   On then, Hieronimo; farewell till soon.
HIERONIMO.
   You'll ply this gear?
LORENZO.   I warrant you.   *Exeunt all but* Hieronimo.
HIERONIMO.   Why so!
   Now shall I see the fall of Babylon,   190
   Wrought by the heavens in this confusion.
   And if the world like not this tragedy,
   Hard is the hap of old Hieronimo.   *Exit.*

[IV.ii]   *Enter* Isabella *with a weapon.*

ISABELLA.
   Tell me no more! —Oh, monstrous homicides!
   Since neither piety nor pity moves
   The king to justice or compassion,
   I will revenge myself upon this place,
   Where thus they murdered my beloved son.   5
                          She cuts down the arbor.
   Down with these branches and these loathsome boughs
   Of this unfortunate and fatal pine!
   Down with them, Isabella; rent them up,
   And burn the roots from whence the rest is sprung!
   I will not leave a root, a stalk, a tree,   10
   A bough, a branch, a blossom, nor a leaf,
   No, not an herb within this garden plot,

---

1. S.P. ISABELLA.] *edd.; not in Qq.*

---

   187. *soothe . . . up*] indulge his humors or whims.
   189. *ply this gear*] proceed with this business.
   190. *the fall of Babylon*] Revelation 18; or referring to the Tower of Babel? (E).

THE SPANISH TRAGEDY   IV.iii

Accursed complot of my misery!
Fruitless forever may this garden be,
Barren the earth, and blissless whosoever   15
Imagines not to keep it unmanur'd!
An eastern wind, commix'd with noisome airs,
Shall blast the plants and the young saplings;
The earth with serpents shall be pestered,
And passengers, for fear to be infect,   20
Shall stand aloof, and, looking at it, tell:
"There, murder'd, died the son of Isabel."
Ay, here he died, and here I him embrace!
See, where his ghost solicits with his wounds
Revenge on her that should revenge his death.   25
Hieronimo, make haste to see thy son;
For sorrow and despair hath cited me
To hear Horatio plead with Rhadamanth.
Make haste, Hieronimo, to hold excus'd
Thy negligence in pursuit of their deaths   30
Whose hateful wrath bereav'd him of his breath.
Ah, nay, thou dost delay their deaths,
Forgives the murderers of thy noble son,
And none but I bestir me—to no end!
And as I curse this tree from further fruit,   35
So shall my womb be cursed for his sake;
And with this weapon will I wound the breast,
The hapless breast, that gave Horatio suck.   *She stabs herself.*

[IV.iii]
Enter Hieronimo; *he knocks up the curtain. Enter the* Duke of Castile.

CASTILE.
  How now, Hieronimo, where's your fellows,
  That you take all this pain?
HIERONIMO.
  Oh sir, it is for the author's credit

38. S.D.] *Q 4–10; after l. 37 in Q 1–3.*

---

13. *complot*] (*a*) garden plot; (*b*) accomplice.
16. *unmanur'd*] uncultivated.
20. *passengers*] travelers.

–163–

IV.iii   THE SPANISH TRAGEDY

    To look that all things may go well.
    But, good my lord, let me entreat your grace 5
    To give the king the copy of the play:
    This is the argument of what we show.
CASTILE.
    I will, Hieronimo.
HIERONIMO.
    One thing more, my good lord.
CASTILE.
    What's that? 10
HIERONIMO.
    Let me entreat your grace
    That, when the train are pass'd into the gallery,
    You would vouchsafe to throw me down the key.
CASTILE.
    I will, Hieronimo.   *Exit* Castile.
HIERONIMO.
    What, are you ready, Balthazar? 15
    Bring a chair and a cushion for the king.

        Enter Balthazar, *with a chair.*

    Well done, Balthazar! hang up the title:—
    Our scene is Rhodes;—what, is your beard on?
BALTHAZAR.
    Half on; the other is in my hand.
HIERONIMO.
    Dispatch for shame; are you so long?   *Exit* Balthazar. 20
    Bethink thyself, Hieronimo,
    Recall thy wits, recompt thy former wrongs
    Thou hast received by murder of thy son,
    And lastly, not least, how Isabel,
    Once his mother and thy dearest wife, 25
    All woebegone for him, hath slain herself.
    Behoves thee then, Hieronimo, to be reveng'd.
    The plot is laid of dire revenge!
    On, then, Hieronimo, pursue revenge,
    For nothing wants but acting of revenge.   *Exit* Hieronimo. 30

---

    17. *title*] see Chambers, Vol. III, pp. 126–127, 154.
    22. *recompt*] recount.

[IV.iv]
Enter Spanish King, Viceroy, Duke of Castile, [Don Pedro], *and their train.*

KING.
Now, viceroy, shall we see the tragedy
Of Soliman, the Turkish emperor,
Perform'd of pleasure by your son the prince,
My nephew Don Lorenzo, and my niece.

VICEROY.
Who? Bel-imperia? 5

KING.
Ay, and Hieronimo, our marshal,
At whose request they deign to do't themselves.
These be our pastimes in the court of Spain.
Here, brother, you shall be the book-keeper:
This is the argument of that they show. 10
He giveth him a book.

Gentlemen, this play of Hieronimo, *in sundry languages, was thought good to be set down in English, more largely, for the easier understanding to every public reader.*

Enter Balthazar, Bel-imperia, *and* Hieronimo.

BALTHAZAR.
Bashaw, that Rhodes is ours, yield heavens the honor,
And holy Mahomet, our sacred prophet!
And be thou grac'd with every excellence
That Soliman can give, or thou desire.
But thy desert in conquering Rhodes is less 15
Than in reserving this fair Christian nymph,
Perseda, blissful lamp of excellence,
Whose eyes compel, like powerful adamant,
The warlike heart of Soliman to wait.

KING.
See, viceroy, that is Balthazar, your son, 20
That represents the emperor Soliman:
How well he acts his amorous passion!

---

9. *book-keeper*] prompter.
18. *adamant*] diamond, then confused with the loadstone as being magnetic.

IV.iv   THE SPANISH TRAGEDY

VICEROY.
Ay, Bel-imperia hath taught him that.
CASTILE.
That's because his mind runs all on Bel-imperia.
HIERONIMO.
Whatever joy earth yields, betide your majesty.   25
BALTHAZAR.
Earth yields no joy without Perseda's love.
HIERONIMO.
Let then Perseda on your grace attend.
BALTHAZAR.
She shall not wait on me, but I on her:
Drawn by the influence of her lights, I yield.
But let my friend, the Rhodian knight, come forth,   30
Erasto, dearer than my life to me,
That he may see Perseda, my beloved.

Enter Erasto.

KING.
Here comes Lorenzo: look upon the plot,
And tell me, brother, what part plays he?
BEL-IMPERIA.
Ah, my Erasto, welcome to Perseda.   35
LORENZO.
Thrice happy is Erasto that thou livest;
Rhodes' loss is nothing to Erasto's joy;
Sith his Perseda lives, his life survives.
BALTHAZAR.
Ah, bashaw, here is love between Erasto
And fair Perseda, sovereign of my soul.   40
HIERONIMO.
Remove Erasto, mighty Soliman,
And then Perseda will be quickly won.
BALTHAZAR.
Erasto is my friend; and while he lives,
Perseda never will remove her love.
HIERONIMO.
Let not Erasto live to grieve great Soliman.   45

39. between] *Qq*; betwixt *B*.

-166-

THE SPANISH TRAGEDY   IV.iv

BALTHAZAR.
   Dear is Erasto in our princely eye.
HIERONIMO.
   But if he be your rival, let him die.
BALTHAZAR.
   Why, let him die—so love commandeth me;
   Yet grieve I that Erasto should so die.
HIERONIMO.
   Erasto, Soliman saluteth thee,   50
   And lets thee wit by me his highness' will,
   Which is, thou shouldst be thus employ'd.   *Stab him.*
BEL-IMPERIA.   *Ay me!*
   Erasto! See, Soliman; Erasto's slain!
BALTHAZAR.
   Yet liveth Soliman to comfort thee.
   Fair queen of beauty, let not favor die,   55
   But with a gracious eye behold his grief,
   That with Perseda's beauty is increas'd,
   If by Perseda his grief be not releas'd.
BEL-IMPERIA.
   Tyrant, desist soliciting vain suits;
   Relentless are mine ears to thy laments,   60
   As thy butcher is pitiless and base,
   Which seiz'd on my Erasto, harmless knight.
   Yet by thy power thou thinkest to command,
   And to thy power Perseda doth obey;
   But, were she able, thus she would revenge   65
   Thy treacheries on thee, ignoble prince: *Stab him.*
   And on herself she would be thus reveng'd.   *Stab herself.*
KING.
   Well said! —Old Marshal, this was bravely done!
HIERONIMO.
   But Bel-imperia plays Perseda well!
VICEROY.
   Were this in earnest, Bel-imperia,   70
   You would be better to my son than so.

58. *Perseda his*] *S; Persedaes Qq.*

---

68. *Well said!*] Well done!

−167−

IV.iv   The Spanish Tragedy

KING.
>But now what follows for Hieronimo?

HIERONIMO.
>Marry, this follows for Hieronimo;
>Here break we off our sundry languages,
>And thus conclude I in our vulgar tongue.   75
>Haply you think—but bootless are your thoughts—
>That this is fabulously counterfeit,
>And that we do as all tragedians do:
>To die today (for fashioning our scene)
>The death of Ajax or some Roman peer,   80
>And in a minute, starting up again,
>Revive to please tomorrow's audience.
>No, princes; know I am Hieronimo,
>The hopeless father of a hapless son,
>Whose tongue is tun'd to tell his latest tale,   85
>Not to excuse gross errors in the play.
>I see your looks urge instance of these words;
>Behold the reason urging me to this!   *Shows his dead son.*
>See here my show; look on this spectacle!
>Here lay my hope, and here my hope hath end!   90
>Here lay my heart, and here my heart was slain!
>Here lay my treasure, here my treasure lost!
>Here lay my bliss, and here my bliss bereft!
>But hope, heart, treasure, joy, and bliss,
>All fled, fail'd, died, yea, all decay'd, with this.   95
>From forth these wounds came breath that gave me life;
>They murder'd me that made these fatal marks.
>The cause was love, whence grew this mortal hate;
>The hate, Lorenzo and young Balthazar;
>The love, my son to Bel-imperia.   100
>But night, the coverer of accursed crimes,
>With pitchy silence hush'd these traitors' harms,
>And lent them leave, for they had sorted leisure
>To take advantage in my garden plot
>Upon my son, my dear Horatio.   105

---

77. *fabulously*] as in a fable; fictitiously.
87. *instance*] example, proof.
103. *sorted*] arranged, selected.

THE SPANISH TRAGEDY   IV.iv

There merciless they butcher'd up my boy,
In black, dark night, to pale, dim, cruel death.
He shrieks; I heard—and yet, methinks, I hear—
His dismal outcry echo in the air.
With soonest speed I hasted to the noise,   110
Where hanging on a tree I found my son,
Through-girt with wounds, and slaughter'd as you see.
And grieved I, think you, at this spectacle?
Speak, Portuguese, whose loss resembles mine:
If thou canst weep upon thy Balthazar,   115
'Tis like I wail'd for my Horatio.—
And you, my lord, whose reconciled son
March'd in a net, and thought himself unseen,
And rated me for brainsick lunacy,
With "God amend that mad Hieronimo!"—   120
How can you brook our play's catastrophe?—
And here behold this bloody handkercher,
Which at Horatio's death I weeping dipp'd
Within the river of his bleeding wounds:
It, as propitious, see, I have reserved,   125
And never hath it left my bloody heart,
Soliciting remembrance of my vow
With these, oh, these accursed murderers!
Which now perform'd, my heart is satisfied.
And to this end the bashaw I became,   130
That might revenge me on Lorenzo's life,
Who therefore was appointed to the part,
And was to represent the knight of Rhodes,
That I might kill him more conveniently.
So, viceroy, was this Balthazar, thy son,   135
That Soliman which Bel-imperia,
In person of Perseda, murdered,
Solely appointed to that tragic part
That she might slay him that offended her.
Poor Bel-imperia miss'd her part in this;   140
For though the story saith she should have died,

112. *girt*] pierced.
118. *March'd in a net*] acted without concealment, while pretending to escape notice.
121. *brook*] endure.

−169−

IV.iv   THE SPANISH TRAGEDY

> Yet I of kindness, and of care to her,
> Did otherwise determine of her end;
> But love of him whom they did hate too much
> Did urge her resolution to be such. 145
> And, princes, now behold Hieronimo,
> Author and actor in this tragedy,
> Bearing his latest fortune in his fist;
> And will as resolute conclude his part
> As any of the actors gone before. 150
> And, gentles, thus I end my play;
> Urge no more words—I have no more to say.
>
> *He runs to hang himself.*

KING.
> Oh hearken, viceroy!—Hold, Hieronimo!
> Brother, my nephew and thy son are slain!

VICEROY.
> We are betray'd; my Balthazar is slain! 155
> Break ope the doors; run, save Hieronimo.
>
> [*They break in and hold* Hieronimo.]
>
> Hieronimo, do but inform the king of these events;
> Upon mine honor, thou shalt have no harm.

HIERONIMO.
> Viceroy, I will not trust thee with my life,
> Which I this day have offered to my son.— 160
> Accursed wretch,
> Why stayest thou him that was resolv'd to die?

KING.
> Speak, traitor! damned, bloody murderer, speak!
> For now I have thee, I will make thee speak.
> Why hast thou done this undeserving deed? 165

VICEROY.
> Why hast thou murdered my Balthazar?

CASTILE.
> Why hast thou butchered both my children thus?

HIERONIMO.
> Oh, good words! As dear to me was my Horatio,
> As yours, or yours, or yours, my lord, to you.

156.1.] *Q 4–10; not in Q 1–3.*

---

156. *Break ope*] since they are locked in. See IV.iii.12-13.

−170−

THE SPANISH TRAGEDY   IV.iv

 My guiltless son was by Lorenzo slain,   170
 And by Lorenzo and that Balthazar
 Am I at last revenged thoroughly,
 Upon whose souls may heavens be yet avenged
 With greater far than these afflictions.
CASTILE.
 But who were thy confederates in this?   175
VICEROY.
 That was thy daughter, Bel-imperia;
 For by her hand my Balthazar was slain:
 I saw her stab him.
KING.   Why speakest thou not?
HIERONIMO.
 What lesser liberty can kings afford
 Than harmless silence? Then afford it me.   180
 Sufficeth, I may not, nor I will not tell thee.
KING.
 Fetch forth the tortures! Traitor as thou art,
 I'll make thee tell.
HIERONIMO.   Indeed,
 Thou mayest torment me as his wretched son
 Hath done in murd'ring my Horatio;   185
 But never shalt thou force me to reveal
 The thing which I have vow'd inviolate.
 And therefore, in despite of all thy threats,
 Pleas'd with their deaths, and eas'd with their revenge,
 First take my tongue, and afterwards my heart. 190

    [Fifth passage of additions.]
[HIERONIMO.
 But are you sure they are dead?   (*168*)
CASTILE.
 Ay, slave, too sure.
HIERONIMO.
 What, and yours too?   (*170*)
VICEROY.
 Ay, all are dead; not one of them survive.

(*168*)–(*217.1*). HIERONIMO. But . . . *ll. 168–178* (. . . stab him) *and l. 190*
tongue.] *Q 4–10, replacing ll. 168–190,* *of the original text.*
but incorporating, in transposed order,

−171−

IV.iv   THE SPANISH TRAGEDY

HIERONIMO.
>   Nay, then I care not; come, and we shall be friends;
>   Let us lay our heads together:
>   See, here's a goodly noose will hold them all.

VICEROY.
>   Oh damned devil, how secure he is!   (*175*)

HIERONIMO.
>   Secure? Why, dost thou wonder at it?
>   I tell thee, viceroy, this day I have seen revenge,
>   And in that sight am grown a prouder monarch
>   Than ever sat under the crown of Spain.
>   Had I as many lives as there be stars,   (*180*)
>   As many heavens to go to, as those lives,
>   I'd give them all, ay, and my soul to boot,
>   But I would see thee ride in this red pool.

CASTILE.
>   Speak, who were thy confederates in this?

VICEROY.
>   That was thy daughter Bel-imperia;   (*185*)
>   For by her hand my Balthazar was slain:
>   I saw her stab him.

HIERONIMO.
>   Oh, good words! As dear to me was my Horatio,
>   As yours, or yours, or yours, my lord, to you.
>   My guiltless son was by Lorenzo slain,   (*190*)
>   And by Lorenzo and that Balthazar
>   Am I at last revenged thoroughly,
>   Upon whose souls may heavens be yet revenged
>   With greater far than these afflictions.
>   Methinks, since I grew inward with revenge,   (*195*)
>   I cannot look with scorn enough on death.

KING.
>   What, dost thou mock us, slave? —Bring tortures forth!

HIERONIMO.
>   Do, do, do; and meantime I'll torture you.
>   You had a son, as I take it; and your son

    (*175*). *secure*] carefree, arrogant.
    (*180–183*).] from Marlowe's *Doctor Faustus*, ll. 337–338: "Had I as many soules as there be starres,/ Ide giue them al for Mephastophilis."
    (*195*). *inward*] intimate.

Should ha' been married to your daughter. (200)
Ha, was't not so? —You had a son, too;
He was my liege's nephew. He was proud
And politic; had he lived, he might 'a' come
To wear the crown of Spain. I think 'twas so—
'Twas I that killed him; look you, this same hand, (205)
'Twas it that stabb'd his heart—do ye see? this hand—
For one Horatio, if you ever knew him: a youth,
One that they hanged up in his father's garden;
One that did force your valiant son to yield,
While your more valiant son did take him prisoner. (210)

VICEROY.
Be deaf, my senses; I can hear no more.

KING.
Fall, heaven, and cover us with thy sad ruins.

CASTILE.
Roll all the world within thy pitchy cloud.

HIERONIMO.
Now do I applaud what I have acted.
Nunc iners cadat manus! (215)
Now to express the rupture of my part—
First take my tongue, and afterward my heart.
He bites out his tongue.]

KING.
Oh monstrous resolution of a wretch! 191 (218)
See, viceroy, he hath bitten forth his tongue,
Rather than to reveal what we requir'd.

CASTILE.
Yet can he write.

KING.
And if in this he satisfy us not, 195 (222)
We will devise th' extremest kind of death
That ever was invented for a wretch.

Then he makes signs for a knife to mend his pen.

(215). iners cadat] S; mors caede Q4;
mers cadae Q5-8; mens cadae Q9-10.

---

(215).] "Now may my hand fall idle!"
(216). rupture] breaking.

−173−

IV.iv   THE SPANISH TRAGEDY

CASTILE.
  Oh, he would have a knife to mend his pen.
VICEROY.
  Here, and advise thee that thou write the troth.
KING.
  Look to my brother! save Hieronimo!   200   (227)
       He with a knife stabs the Duke *and himself.*
  What age hath ever heard such monstrous deeds?
  My brother, and the whole succeeding hope
  That Spain expected after my decease!
  Go, bear his body hence, that we may mourn
  The loss of our beloved brother's death,   205   (232)
  That he may be entomb'd, whate'er befall.
  I am the next, the nearest, last of all.
VICEROY.
  And thou, Don Pedro, do the like for us;
  Take up our hapless son, untimely slain;
  Set me with him, and he with woeful me,   210   (237)
  Upon the mainmast of a ship unmann'd,
  And let the wind and tide haul me along
  To Scylla's barking and untamed gulf,
  Or to the loathsome pool of Acheron,
  To weep my want for my sweet Balthazar;   215   (242)
  Spain hath no refuge for a Portingale.

The trumpets sound a dead march; the King of Spain *mourning after his brother's body, and the* King of Portingale *bearing the body of his son.*

[IV.v]   [CHORUS]
GHOST.
  Ay, now my hopes have end in their effects,
  When blood and sorrow finish my desires:
  Horatio murdered in his father's bower;
  Vile Serberine by Pedringano slain;
  False Pedringano hang'd by quaint device;   5
  Fair Isabella by herself misdone;

200–201. KING. Look.../ What]   213. gulf] *Q 9–10;* greefe *Q 1–8.*
edd.; Look.../ *King.* What...   IV.v.0.1.] *edd.;* Enter Ghoast *and*
Qq, S.   Reuenge. *Qq.*

5. *quaint*] crafty, ingenious.   6. *misdone*] killed.

−174−

Prince Balthazar by Bel-imperia stabb'd;
The Duke of Castile and his wicked son
Both done to death by old Hieronimo;
My Bel-imperia fallen as Dido fell,   10
And good Hieronimo slain by himself:
Ay, these were spectacles to please my soul.
Now will I beg at lovely Proserpine
That, by the virtue of her princely doom,
I may consort my friends in pleasing sort,   15
And on my foes work just and sharp revenge.
I'll lead my friend Horatio through those fields
Where never-dying wars are still inur'd;
I'll lead fair Isabella to that train
Where pity weeps, but never feeleth pain;   20
I'll lead my Bel-imperia to those joys
That vestal virgins and fair queens possess;
I'll lead Hieronimo where Orpheus plays,
Adding sweet pleasure to eternal days.—
But say, Revenge, for thou must help, or none,   25
Against the rest how shall my hate be shown?

REVENGE.
  This hand shall hale them down to deepest hell,
  Where none but Furies, bugs, and tortures dwell.

GHOST.
  Then, sweet Revenge, do this at my request:
  Let me be judge, and doom them to unrest.   30
  Let loose poor Tityus from the vulture's gripe,
  And let Don Cyprian supply his room;
  Place Don Lorenzo on Ixion's wheel,
  And let the lovers' endless pains surcease
  (Juno forgets old wrath, and grants him ease);   35
  Hang Balthazar about Chimaera's neck,
  And let him there bewail his bloody love,

---

18. *inur'd*] practiced.
19. *train*] way of life.
28. *bugs*] bugbears, objects of terror.
32.] Note the treatment of Don Cyprian; cf. Introduction, p. xxviii.
33. *Ixion*] who had tried to seduce Juno.
34. *surcease*] end.
36. *Chimaera*] a fire-breathing monster.

IV.v   THE SPANISH TRAGEDY

    Repining at our joys that are above;
    Let Serberine go roll the fatal stone,
    And take from Sisyphus his endless moan;   40
    False Pedringano, for his treachery,
    Let him be dragg'd through boiling Acheron,
    And there live, dying still in endless flames,
    Blaspheming gods and all their holy names.
REVENGE.
    Then haste we down to meet thy friends and foes: 45
    To place thy friends in ease, the rest in woes;
    For here though death hath end their misery.
    I'll there begin their endless tragedy.   *Exeunt.*

Appendix

Chronology

Approximate years are indicated by *, occurrences in doubt by (?).

Political and Literary Events	*Life and Major Works of Kyd*
1558 Accession of Queen Elizabeth I. Robert Greene born.	Thomas Kyd born in London; baptized November 6.
1560 George Chapman born.	
1561 Francis Bacon born.	
1564 Shakespeare born. Christopher Marlowe born.	
1565	Entered at Merchant Taylors' School, London.
1570 Thomas Heywood born.*	
1572 Thomas Dekker born.* John Donne born. Massacre of St. Bartholomew's Day.	
1573 Ben Jonson born.*	
1576 The Theatre, the first permanent public theater in London, established by James Burbage. John Marston born.	
1577 The Curtain theater opened.	

−177−

Appendix

Holinshed's *Chronicles of England, Scotland and Ireland*.
Drake begins circumnavigation of the earth; completed 1580.
1578
John Lyly's *Euphues: The Anatomy of Wit*.
1579
John Fletcher born.
Sir Thomas North's translation of Plutarch's *Lives*.
Spenser's *The Shepheardes Calender* published.
1580
Spain incorporates Portugal.
Thomas Middleton born.
1581
Thomas Newton, *Seneca his tenne Tragedies translated into Englysh*.
1582
Thomas Watson's *Hecatompathia* published.
1583
The Queen's Men formed.
Philip Massinger born.
1584
Francis Beaumont born.*
George Peele's *The Arraignment of Paris* published.
1585
Robert Garnier's collected plays published.
1586
Death of Sir Philip Sidney.
John Ford born.
1587
The Rose theater opened by Henslowe.
Marlowe's *TAMBURLAINE*, Part I.*
Execution of Mary, Queen of Scots.
Drake raids Cadiz.

THE FIRST PART OF HIERONIMO written.*

THE SPANISH TRAGEDY written.*

*SOLIMAN AND PERSEDA.**
Entered the service of Lord Pembroke.*

-178-

CHRONOLOGY

1588
Defeat of the Spanish Armada.
Marlowe's *TAMBURLAINE*, Part II.*

The Housholders Philosophie (translation of Tasso's *Il Padre de Famiglia*).

1589
Greene's *Menaphon* published, with Nashe's attack (in the *Epistle*) on Kyd and *Hamlet*.
Greene's *FRIAR BACON AND FRIAR BUNGAY*.*
Marlowe's *THE JEW OF MALTA*.*

1590
Spenser's *Faerie Queene* (Books I–III) published.
Sidney's *Arcadia* published.
Shakespeare's *HENRY VI*, Parts I–III,* *TITUS ANDRONICUS*.*

1591
Shakespeare's *RICHARD III*.*

Writing with Marlowe "in one chamber."

1592
Arden of Faversham published.
Marlowe's *DOCTOR FAUSTUS** and *EDWARD II*.*
Shakespeare's *TAMING OF THE SHREW** and *THE COMEDY OF ERRORS*.*
Death of Greene.

THE SPANISH TRAGEDY printed.
SOLIMAN AND PERSEDA printed.*

1593
Shakespeare's *LOVE'S LABOR'S LOST;** *Venus and Adonis* published.
Marlowe arrested.
Death of Marlowe, June 1.
Theaters closed on account of plague.

Arrested May 12.
Letter to Puckering.

1594
Shakespeare's *TWO GENTLEMEN OF VERONA;** *The Rape of Lucrece* published.
Shakespeare's company becomes Lord Chamberlain's Men.

Translation of Robert Garnier's *Cornélie* printed.
Death of Kyd.

–179–

APPENDIX

1595
The Swan theater built.
Sidney's *Defense of Poesy* published.
Shakespeare's *ROMEO AND JULIET,* A MIDSUMMER NIGHT'S DREAM,* RICHARD II.*
Raleigh's first expedition to Guiana.

1596
Spenser's *Faerie Queene* (Books IV–VI) published.
Shakespeare's *MERCHANT OF VENICE,* KING JOHN.*
James Shirley born.

1597
Bacon's *Essays* (first edition).
Shakespeare's *HENRY IV*, Part I.*

1598
Demolition of The Theatre.
Shakespeare's *MUCH ADO ABOUT NOTHING,* HENRY IV*, Part II.*
Jonson's *EVERY MAN IN HIS HUMOR* (first version).
Seven books of Chapman's translation of Homer's *Iliad* published.

1599
The Paul's Boys reopen their theater.
The Globe theater opened.
Shakespeare's *AS YOU LIKE IT,* HENRY V, JULIUS CAESAR.*
Marston's *ANTONIO AND MELLIDA,* Parts I and II.
Dekker's *THE SHOEMAKERS' HOLIDAY.*
Death of Spenser.

1600
Shakespeare's *TWELFTH NIGHT.*
The Fortune theater built by Alleyn.

Chronology

The Children of the Chapel begin to play at the Blackfriars.

1601
Shakespeare's *HAMLET*,* *MERRY WIVES OF WINDSOR*.*
Insurrection and execution of the Earl of Essex.
Jonson's *POETASTER*.

Ben Jonson paid for "Additions" to *THE SPANISH TRAGEDY* (1601, 1602).

1602
Shakespeare's *TROILUS AND CRESSIDA*.*

1603
HAMLET, Q1, published.
Death of Queen Elizabeth I; accession of James VI of Scotland as James I.
Florio's translation of Montaigne's *Essays* published.
Shakespeare's *ALL'S WELL THAT ENDS WELL*.*
Heywood's *A WOMAN KILLED WITH KINDNESS*.
Marston's *THE MALCONTENT*.*
Shakespeare's company becomes the King's Men.

1604
HAMLET, Q2, published.
Shakespeare's *MEASURE FOR MEASURE*,* *OTHELLO*.*
Marston's *THE FAWN*.*
Chapman's *BUSSY D'AMBOIS*.*

THE FIRST PART OF HIERONIMO misappropriated by The Children of the Chapel.

1605
Shakespeare's *KING LEAR*.*
Marston's *THE DUTCH COURTESAN*.*
Bacon's *Advancement of Learning* published.
The Gunpowder Plot.

THE FIRST PART OF HIERONIMO published.

1606
Shakespeare's *MACBETH*.*
Jonson's *VOLPONE*.*

Appendix

Tourneur's *REVENGER'S TRAG-
EDY.*
The Red Bull theater built.
Death of John Lyly.

1607
Shakespeare's *ANTONY AND
CLEOPATRA.*
Beaumont's *KNIGHT OF THE
BURNING PESTLE.*
Settlement of Jamestown, Virginia.

1608
Shakespeare's *CORIOLANUS,*
TIMON OF ATHENS,* PERI-
CLES.*
Chapman's *CONSPIRACY AND
TRAGEDY OF CHARLES, DUKE
OF BYRON.*
Dekker's *Gull's Hornbook* published.
Richard Burbage leases Blackfriars theater for King's company.
John Milton born.

1609
Shakespeare's *CYMBELINE;*
Sonnets* published.
Jonson's *EPICOENE.*

1610
Jonson's *ALCHEMIST.*
Chapman's *REVENGE OF BUSSY
D'AMBOIS.*
Richard Crashaw born.

1611
Authorized (King James) Version of the Bible published.
Shakespeare's *THE WINTER'S
TALE,* THE TEMPEST.*
Beaumont and Fletcher's *A KING
AND NO KING.*
Middleton's *A CHASTE MAID IN
CHEAPSIDE.*
Tourneur's *ATHEIST'S TRAG-
EDY.*
Chapman's translation of *Iliad* completed.

Chronology

1612
Webster's THE WHITE DEVIL.*

1613
The Globe theater burned.
Shakespeare's HENRY VIII (with Fletcher).
Webster's THE DUCHESS OF MALFI.*
Sir Thomas Overbury murdered.

1614
The Globe theater rebuilt.
The Hope theater built.
Jonson's BARTHOLOMEW FAIR.

1616
Publication of Folio edition of Jonson's *Works*.
Chapman's *Whole Works of Homer*.
Death of Shakespeare.
Death of Beaumont.

1618
Outbreak of Thirty Years War.
Execution of Raleigh.

1620
Settlement of Plymouth, Massachusetts.

1621
Middleton's WOMEN BEWARE WOMEN.*
Robert Burton's *Anatomy of Melancholy* published.
Andrew Marvell born.

1622
Middleton and Rowley's THE CHANGELING.*
Henry Vaughan born.

1623
Publication of Folio edition of Shakespeare's COMEDIES, HISTORIES, AND TRAGEDIES.

1625
Death of King James I; accession of Charles I.
Death of Fletcher.

Appendix

1626
Death of Tourneur.
Death of Bacon.

1627
Death of Middleton.

1628
Ford's *THE LOVER'S MELAN-CHOLY*.
Petition of Right.
Buckingham assassinated.

1631
Shirley's *THE TRAITOR*.
Death of Donne.
John Dryden born.

1632
Massinger's *THE CITY MAD-AM*.*

1633
Donne's *Poems* published.
Death of George Herbert.

1634
Death of Chapman, Marston, Webster.*
Publication of *THE TWO NOBLE KINSMEN*, with title-page attribution to Shakespeare and Fletcher.
Milton's *Comus*.

1635
Sir Thomas Browne's *Religio Medici*.

1637
Death of Jonson.

1639
First Bishops' War.
Death of Carew.*

1640
Short Parliament.
Long Parliament impeaches Laud.
Death of Massinger, Burton.

1641
Irish rebel.
Death of Heywood.

CHRONOLOGY

1642
Charles I leaves London; Civil War breaks out.
Shirley's *COURT SECRET*.
All theaters closed by Act of Parliament.

1643
Parliament swears to the Solemn League and Covenant.

1645
Ordinance for New Model Army enacted.

1646
End of First Civil War.

1647
Army occupies London.
Charles I forms alliance with Scots.
Publication of Folio edition of Beaumont and Fletcher's *COMEDIES AND TRAGEDIES*.

1648
Second Civil War.

1649
Execution of Charles I.

1650
Jeremy Collier born.

1651
Hobbes' *Leviathan* published.

1652
First Dutch War began (ended 1654).
Thomas Otway born.

1653
Nathaniel Lee born.*

1656
D'Avenant's *THE SIEGE OF RHODES* performed at Rutland House.

1657
John Dennis born.

Appendix

1658
Death of Oliver Cromwell.
D'Avenant's *THE CRUELTY OF THE SPANIARDS IN PERU* performed at the Cockpit.

1660
Restoration of Charles II.
Theatrical patents granted to Thomas Killigrew and Sir William D'Avenant, authorizing them to form, respectively, the King's and the Duke of York's Companies.

1661
Cowley's *THE CUTTER OF COLEMAN STREET*.
D'Avenant's *THE SIEGE OF RHODES* (expanded to two parts).

1662
Charter granted to the Royal Society.

1663
Dryden's *THE WILD GALLANT*.
Tuke's *THE ADVENTURES OF FIVE HOURS*.

1664
Sir John Vanbrugh born.
Dryden's *THE RIVAL LADIES*.
Dryden and Howard's *THE INDIAN QUEEN*.
Etherege's *THE COMICAL REVENGE*.

1665
Second Dutch War began (ended 1667).
Great Plague.
Dryden's *THE INDIAN EMPEROR*.
Orrery's *MUSTAPHA*.

1666
Fire of London.
Death of James Shirley.